MISSOURI HANDBOOK NUMBER FOUR

THE COMMON FOSSILS OF MISSOURI

A. G. UNKLESBAY

UNIVERSITY OF MISSOURI PRESS • COLUM

T0170843

ACKNOWLEDGMENT

Acknowledgment is made to Missouri's noted paleontologists whose research has provided much of the material for this handbook and to the inspiration resulting from the enthusiasm and interest of high school students, teachers, and amateur paleontologists of Missouri.

Dr. R. E. Peck and other staff members of the Department of Geology of the University of Missouri as well as Dr. T. R. Beveridge and Dr. Wally Howe and other members of the staff of the Missouri Geologic Survey have given valued encouragement.

Acknowledgement is also due Harold Levin and Floyd Twenter who prepared the drawings; Wendell Cochran who drafted the map; and Kenneth Larsen and Roy Hatcher who made many of the photographs. The cover photograph is by John Gerard.

CONTENTS

LIST OF ILLUSTRATIONS

INTRODUCTION

Since the days of pre-historic man unusual rocks and fossil specimens have been objects of interest and curiosity for many fossil and rock collections have been found with the remains of the early cave dwellers.

Just what pre-historic man thought of such objects is not known, but we do know that for centuries men have wondered about them and have had many different ideas concerning their origin. For many years they were thought to be special creations, or freaks or sports of nature until it became known that many of these forms actually represent once-living creatures. Little by little more has been learned about these ancient life forms known as fossils.

The discovery and study of fossils has become the important science of Paleontology. This science has followers ranging from amateurs who pursue it as a hobby, to professional men who devote their lives to studying fossils, and using them as aids in finding oil and other mineral resources. A knowledge of fossils also helps interpret the history of the earth.

Fossils range in size from minute forms which can only be seen through a microscope to the skeletal remains of the giant dinosaurs reaching as much as 90 feet in length and as much as 45 tons in weight. So complex is paleontology that many scientists may spend the greater part of their lives gathering data on some very small part of the fossilized plant or animal kingdoms.

Fossils are plentiful in many of the rock formations in Missouri and when properly understood their presence reveals many fascinating details about the geologic history of the state. Because Missourians have shown their interest in these fossils through numerous requests for information to the State Geological Survey and to the geology departments of the educational institutions in the state, this report was prepared. It is for these interested people and for others who may become interested.

Because it is difficult to understand the life of the past without some appreciation of the life of the present, this Handbook includes a brief introduction to the modern forms whose ancestors and relatives are represented in the fossil record.

WHAT IS A FOSSIL?

The word fossil is derived from Latin and means "to dig" or "to be dug up." For many years the word was applied to any solid object dug out of a rock formation, but it is now used as a name for those things buried in the rocks which are evidence for the existence of life in the geologic past, and give some idea of the size, shape, and form, or other feature of a once living animal or plant.

Many fossils represent shellfish or other animals that lived in seas, lakes, or rivers, and were buried in the mud or sand. Others represent animals that were mired in the mud of swamps or river flood plains. Also fossils may be impressions, or remains, of plants whose leaves or stems fell to the ground and were covered by mud and sand.

Many fossils have been buried for millions of years, and a study of them determines what life was like in the ages that have gone before us.

GEOLOGIC HISTORY

Life has existed on the earth for many millions of years, and throughout these many ages living things have been constantly changing. Many forms have become extinct and many new ones have arisen. It is not known exactly why or how some of these changes took place, but it seems fairly certain that many were in response to changes in the conditions under which the life existed. Certain forms became adapted to certain environments and changes in the environment were reflected by changes in the plants and animals. By interpreting the fossilized remains of plants and animals much of the ancient history of environmental changes of our planet can be reconstructed.

Throughout these millions of years a trend toward increasing complexity in the history of many groups can be detected. It is only reasonable then to assume that, with an understanding of these groups, the relative degree of complexity of any member of the group will give some measure of its relative age. It follows that by combining an understanding of the development of the plants and animals with an interpretation of their past environments we can begin to write some sort of history of the events of the geologic past. A pictorial representation of the earth's geologic history is shown in Figure 1.

In this history we divide geologic time into units called Eras, and

GEOLOGIC TIME CHART

TIME UNITS			YEARS AGO	CHARACTERISTIC LIFE
CENOZOIC ERA	CENOZOIC PERIOD	PLEISTOCENE EPOCH	1,000,000	MODERN FORMS OF LIFE DEVELOPED
		PLIOCENE EPOCH	12,000,000	
		MIOCENE EPOCH	26,000,000	
		OLIGOCENE EPOCH	38,000,000	
		EOCENE EPOCH	45,000,000	
		PALEOCENE EPOCH	58,000,000	
MESOZOIC ERA	CRETACEOUS PERIOD		127,000,000	APPEARANCE OF FLOWERING PLANTS DINOSAURS COMMON
	JURASSIC PERIOD		152,000,000	MANY GANOID FISHES FIRST BIRDS DINOSAURS
	TRIASSIC PERIOD		182,000,000	FIRST MAMMALS AMPHIBIANS, REPTILES, AND FISHES
PALEOZOIC ERA	PERMIAN PERIOD		203,000,000	REPTILES DIVERSIFY AMPHIBIANS INSECTS MOLLUSCA
	PENNSYLVANIAN PERIOD		225,000,000	COAL PLANTS FIRST REPTILES FIRST INSECTS MOLLUSCA
	MISSISSIPPIAN PERIOD		255,000,000	SHARKS GREAT DEVELOPMENT OF CRINOIDS COAL PLANTS
	DEVONIAN PERIOD		313,000,000	"AGE OF FISHES" PRIMITIVE AMPHIBIANS FIRST FORESTS BRACHIOPODS
	SILURIAN PERIOD		350,000,000	FIRST CORAL REEFS CRINOIDS ABUNDANT FIRST SCORPIONS AND AIR-BREATHING VERTEBRATES
	ORDOVICIAN PERIOD		430,000,000	RISE OF CEPHALOPODS FIRST PRIMITIVE FISH CRINOIDS GASTROPODS
	CAMBRIAN PERIOD		510,000,000	TRILOBITES BRACHIOPODS SPONGES
PRE-CAMBRIAN ERAS			3,350,000,000	INDICATIONS OF LOW FORMS OF ANIMALS AND PLANTS ALGAE

Figure 1. Generalized geologic time chart showing major subdivisions of time, and typical representatives of the life of the time.

we apply names to them which are based on the stage of development of the life of the time. These names which may seem strange at first sight are really very simple. The latter part of each word is zoic which means life, and the first parts of the words denote the stage of development of the life. Paleo means ancient, Meso means middle, and Ceno means recent. Thus when we use Cenozoic we are referring to the time during which the life was more like that of recent time. The Cenozoic Era includes approximately the last 60 million years, the Mesozoic the 120 million years before that, and the Paleozoic extends back to about 550 million years ago. The time before that was a time of only primitive life which is not well preserved as fossils. We sometimes refer to that time simply as pre-Cambrian, or we may divide it into two Eras the Proterozoic (the dawn of life) and the Archeozoic (the time of archaic life.) We are not sure of the length of these eras but they must extend back to at least 4 billion years.

The eras since the beginning of the Paleozoic are divided into smaller units called Periods and they derive their names from the areas where rocks of that period were first studied and described. The Cambrian rocks were named for a region in Wales called Cambria; the term Ordovician is derived from a tribe of people called the Ordovici who once inhabited the part of Wales where these rocks were named. Similarly the Silurian rocks were named for the Silures, a tribe which once occupied part of the British Isles where rocks of this age occur. Devonshire, in England, contains the first-studied section of Devonian rocks. The name Mississippian has been applied to the thick sequence of rocks exposed along the Mississippi River between Illinois and Missouri. The coal fields of Pennsylvania contain thick sequences of alternating beds of limestone, shale, coal, and sandstone which have been described as the Pennsylvanian rocks. The name Permian was first applied to the rocks in the province of Perm in the Ural Mountains of Russia.

The name Triassic does not have a geographic meaning but has been applied to rocks of this age in Europe because the rocks of this period may be easily divided into three distinct layers. The Jura Mountains are composed of the thick sequence of rocks which have been called Jurassic. The term Cretaceous does not have a place of origin because it is derived from the Latin word for chalk Creta. This name has been used because in many parts of the world the rocks of this age are composed of an impure limestone called chalk.

The subdivisions of the Cenozoic have been based on the relationship between the life of that time and of modern times. In these terms the ending cene means recent.

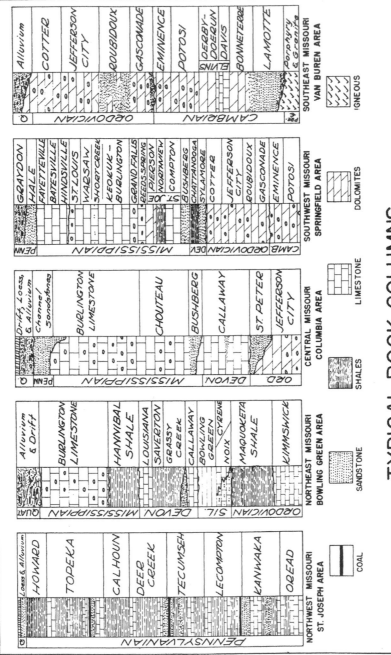

Figure 2. Typical rock columns of different parts of Missouri.

The divisions are as follows:

Pleistocene .... most recent
Pliocene .... more recent
Miocene .... less recent
Oligocene .... little recent
Eocene .... dawn of recent
Paleocene .... ancient recent

FOSSILS AND THE GEOLOGIC TIME SCALE

By studying the fossils of the rocks in the areas for which they were named, and by comparing them with those of other areas, it is possible to get an idea of the relative ages of the rocks and to arrange them in a sort of "standard geologic calendar." This has been done for the world as the simplified version of Figure 1 shows. With this calendar it is then possible to study the fossils in rocks anywhere in the world and to determine their ages by comparison with the standard.

MISSOURI AND THE GEOLOGIC TIME SCALE

Studies such as those mentioned in the preceding section have been made in Missouri, and we now know that this state contains rocks representing all periods shown in Figure 1 except Permian, Triassic, and Jurassic. However, the beds in Missouri are not all continuous over the entire state so one cannot expect to find the complete column represented in any one area. Typical columns in different parts of the state are shown in Figure 2. Not all of the rocks in Missouri contain fossils, but there are many places where they are abundant.

THE FORMATIONS OF MISSOURI

The rocks of Missouri consist largely of two kinds: (1) the igneous rocks such as granite, rhyolite, and porphyry, which are common in the St. Francis Mountains—these rocks were formed by the cooling of great masses of molten rock-making materials; (2) the sedimentary rocks formed by the solidification of accumulations of mud, sand, and gravel. Common sedimentary rocks are conglomerate, sandstone, limestone, dolomite, shale, clay, and coal.[1]   -

Most of the sedimentary rocks were formed in shallow sea water but some of the sandstone and clay accumulated in fresh water. The

---

[1] The rocks and minerals of Missouri are more fully described in Handbook No. 1 of this series by W. D. Keller.

coal accumulated under swamp conditions which were at one time wide-spread in Missouri.

The sedimentary rocks occur in broad extensive layers, almost like blankets spread one upon another to cover the entire state. In general they can be likened to a pile of blankets spread out and then pushed up from below as in the St. Francis Mountain area. While these layers were being pushed up streams flowing over them were eroding valleys and removing large amounts of material. This erosion has gone on to the extent that many formations have been removed from large areas. The granite and porphyry knobs of the Ozark region are places where the entire cover of sedimentary rocks has been removed.

This explanation of the structure of the state is, of course, over-simplified and there are many areas where the blankets are folded, wrinkled, and torn. Also it would be too much to expect any one blanket to extend for long distances without variations in thickness or character. So it is perhaps more nearly correct to compare the sedimentary rocks of the state with a large number of smaller blankets, some of varying thick-ness, some wrinkled and torn, spread in such a way as to cover the state, but with edges overlapping in some places, and not meeting in others. It is obvious that the bottom blankets would have to be put down first and therefore, would be regarded as being older. The same is true of the rocks. The older ones are near the bottom and the younger ones are at the top.

Ages have been assigned to the Missouri rocks by comparison be-tween their fossils and those of a standard geologic calendar. The rocks of the various ages will be briefly discussed here. A detailed discussion would provide material for another book as large as this one.

The approximate distribution of the rocks of various ages is shown on the generalized geologic map (Figure 3).

Pre-Cambrian

The pre-Cambrian rocks of Missouri are almost all igneous. That is, they are rocks which were formed by the cooling of large masses of molten rock deep within the earth. These rocks would not be expected to contain fossils. The prevalent type among these rocks is granite such as is exposed in the St. Francis Mountains in the vicinity of Graniteville. Other types present are rhyolite and porphyry, and some smaller amounts of iron-rich metamorphic rocks. These pre-Cambrian rocks are the oldest rocks in Missouri and presumably underlie the entire state.

Cambrian

The Cambrian rocks of Missouri are all sedimentary rocks which have been formed from sand and mud which accumulated in the seas of

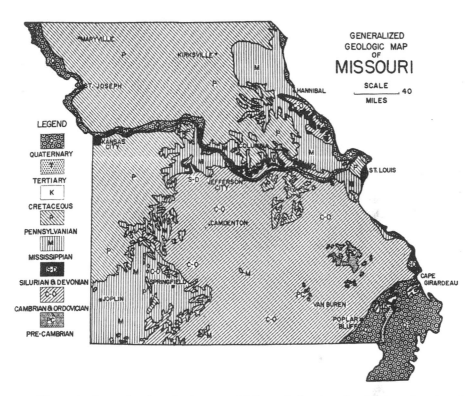

Figure 3. Generalized geologic map of Missouri showing distribution of rocks of various ages.

Late Cambrian time. These rocks now consist dominantly of dolomite, but there are minor amounts of sandstone and shale. The shale and dolomite contain fossils indicating that these beds are of the same age as the type Cambrian beds in Wales. The dolomites in the upper part of the Cambrian section contain large amounts of chert which contains many fossils.

Ordovician

The Ordovician rocks of Missouri are also largely composed of sediments deposited in shallow marine water. The Ordovician section is relatively complete when compared with other parts of the world. The lower part consists mostly of dolomite but there are several prominent sandstone layers. One of these is widely used as building stone in the

Ozark region and it contains some fossil trails and markings. The fossils of the lower part of the Ordovician are mostly in the chert which weathers out of the dolomite formations and mantles the hillsides in the Ozarks.

The middle part of the Ordovician contains the St. Peter sandstone which extends from Illinois to Oklahoma, and from Minnesota to Arkansas. It is quarried and used extensively in making glass at Crystal City. This formation is not known to contain fossils. Above the St. Peter there is a thick sequence of limestones which are exposed in the area from southern Jefferson County northward into Ralls County. These limestones contain many fossils.

The uppermost part of the Ordovician consists largely of shale in which fossils while not rare are not very abundant.

Silurian

The Silurian rocks are almost entirely limestone and they are limited in Missouri to a small area in eastern Cape Girardeau County and to small areas in Lincoln, Pike, and Ralls counties. Fossils are not abundant in these beds but some good ones have been found.

Devonian

The outcrops of Devonian rocks in Missouri are comparatively limited, but rocks of this age are known to underlie a large part of the state. The best exposures are in Cape Girardeau County, and in a narrow band north of the Missouri River from southern Boone County eastward to Warren County. There are also good exposures of Devonian rocks in northeastern Missouri in Pike, Marion, and Ralls counties but the most typical exposures are in southern Callaway County. The Devonian section is mostly of Middle Devonian age and consists mainly of limestone. Some Upper Devonian shale is present.

The Devonian rocks are unusually rich in fossils and there is a great variety of brachiopods and corals. In many areas old coral reefs have been preserved. The Upper Devonian shales contain many conodonts.

Mississippian

The Mississippian rocks of Missouri are part of the type section for this period. They extend in a wide thick layer around the north and west sides of the Ozarks from the Mississippi River to western and southwestern Missouri and continue into Oklahoma and Arkansas. This section contains much shale and limestone, and many beds are particularly rich in fossils. The Burlington limestone is essentially a solid mass of fossils, and many of the limestone, siltstone, and shale beds contain fossils in great abundance. The Northview shale in the southwest and the Hannibal shale in the northeast have been called "worm rocks" because of the great number of worm borings in these beds.

Pennsylvanian

The rocks of the Pennsylvanian contain a greater variety than the rocks of any other period in Missouri. Included in the Pennsylvanian are shale, coal, limestone, sandstone, and clay. The great variety is due to the fact that during Pennsylvanian time there was a great variation in conditions. The seas shifted rapidly and the conditions were constantly changing from marine to non-marine and back again. Much of Missouri was covered with swamp conditions from time to time and in these swamps accumulated much material from which the present day coal beds were formed. Between the periods of swamp conditions, the area was covered with marine water in which limestones were deposited.

The marine limestones contain a great abundance of fossils representing the life of the Pennsylvanian oceans. The coal itself is a record of swamp vegetation and the sandstone and shale beds associated with the coal contain many fossilized ferns and other types of plants.

The Pennsylvanian rocks are very extensive in Missouri and cover much of the area extending from the west-central part of the state northward and eastward to the northern border and continue across the borders into Kansas, Nebraska, and Iowa. In the northern part of the state they are partly covered by glacial material.

Cretaceous

The Cretaceous rocks in Missouri are confined to small areas in Stoddard and Scott counties. They consist mainly of sandstone, but there are also small quantities of sandy clay and a few thin beds of gravel. These beds represent a northern extension of the Gulf of Mexico into Missouri in Cretaceous time. They contain a few poorly preserved marine fossils.

Cenozoic

The Cenozoic rocks of Missouri belong in the Eocene, Pliocene, and Pleistocene. The Eocene rocks are restricted to the southeastern part of the state in Stoddard and Scott counties. The lower part of the section is dominantly clay and the upper part dominantly sand. Fossils are not particularly abundant in these beds but there are some marine invertebrates at the base, and some plant fossils in the upper sand.

The Pliocene is represented by widespread gravel deposits which occur on the tops of many of the high ridges in southeastern Missouri. Their origin is not definitely known but they may represent deposits of the Mississippi River when it was flowing at a much higher level than at present.

The Pleistocene, commonly called the "Ice Age," is represented in Missouri by a widespread blanket of glacial drift which covers much of Missouri north of the Missouri River. This material consists largely of a thoroughly mixed mass of clay, sand, and gravel deposited from the melting glaciers which covered the area within the last million years. Although most of the rocks in the drift are of fairly local origin there are many boulders and pebbles of igneous and metamorphic rocks which the glacier carried down from Canada and Minnesota. In some parts of the area two distinct glacial invasions can be recognized, and in other parts only one is clearly evident. The southern edge of the ice was approximately at the present position of the Missouri River. Along the river, and in part of the area south of the edge of the drift, there are silt and gravel deposits which represent outwash from the melting ice sheet.

THE RECORD OF LIFE IN THE ROCKS

No one knows exactly when life originated on this planet, nor exactly what the first living thing was like. It seems very likely that it was similar to some of our very primitive forms of life as we know them today.

The fossil record of living things begins in the pre-Cambrian rocks, but there the record is rather obscure. We are certain that there were primitive plants (algae) and we have reason to believe that there were simple forms of animal life. Both plants and animals lived in the water.

In the Cambrian rocks the first abundant record of animals is found in the rather complicated forms which bore preservable shells. Among them were trilobites and brachiopods, and probably some sponges and jellyfish.

In the Ordovician the trilobites and brachiopods continued to develop and the brachiopods are still abundant in modern oceans. The trilobites, however, became extinct at the close of the Paleozoic. Cephalopods developed widely in Ordovician time, and along with them came snails and clams which we have in great numbers today. The first good record of vertebrate animals is found in Ordovician rocks where there are considerable numbers of the remains of fish-like forms.

Until the Silurian time the land areas remained barren, but in this period some primitive plants began to grow on land. After the plants began to migrate out of the water they were followed by animals and there is known from Silurian rocks the first record of an air-breathing animal—a small invertebrate creature closely resembling a modern scorpion. It was also in this period that coral reefs developed abundantly and widely. Crinoids were becoming abundant by this time, and many of the other forms already mentioned were continuing to develop.

The meagre beginning of the land plants in the Silurian was only a forerunner of the plants of the Devonian because in this period many areas became forested and land plants grew to large tree-like proportions. Out of the fish-like stock which began in the Ordovician there developed many fish more nearly like our modern ones, and from one of these came a vertebrate creature which developed the ability to crawl out of the water and to breathe air. It was an amphibian, and had to return to water to lay its eggs, but it was the forerunner of many more vertebrates to come.

The Mississippian period saw the continued development of many of the trends which started in the Devonian. There was a wide development of crinoids and blastoids, but the corals and trilobites began to decline. Brachiopods were present in great numbers but began to differ from their ancestors in developing spiny outer surfaces.

The life of the Pennsylvanian is in general an outgrowth of the Mississippian but there were some new developments. One of these was the development of large insects. Imagine, if you can, dragonflies with a two-foot wingspread, and roaches a foot long. They existed in Pennsylvanian swamps. Also in these swamps developed the early reptiles which could lay their eggs out of the water. The plants became widely adapted to swamp life and many forms existed which were not greatly different from those found now in the lush tropical forests.

Physical conditions changed greatly between the Pennsylvanian and the Permian and the changes were reflected in the life. The Permian saw the development of greatly diversified reptiles and greatly diversified plants. Many plants which could stand extreme climatic variation came into existence. Among those were the conifers. Also at this time the insects began the life cycle known as metamorphosis which allows them to survive changes in climate. The close of the Permian brought to an end many of the stocks which had been living since Cambrian time.

The fossil record of land life in the Triassic is not as well preserved as is that of some of the other periods. But, there is no good reason to believe that land plants and animals were any less abundant than in the Jurassic or Cretaceous. The land plants of the Triassic are very similar to those of the coal swamps of the Pennsylvanian, but some new forms, related to modern pines, which grew to diameters of 10 feet and heights of 100 feet, appeared. The land animals included three-toed dinosaurs, and some reptiles which closely resembled crocodiles. In the water grew many swimming reptiles and a large number of invertebrates. The shell-fish were beginning to look more modern, as were the fishes.

Jurassic time saw the development of many large dinosaurs which were probably the largest land animals ever to inhabit the earth. There were also many swimming reptiles and some which learned to fly. From some of the flying ones developed the first birds. Many invertebrates began to develop modern forms and many of the modern insects were present. Marine life was not greatly different from that of the Triassic.

The Cretaceous period was a time of great advancement in the development of land plants with the first appearance of deciduous trees, flowering plants, grasses, and grains. With an abundant source of plant food it was possible for the mammals, which had been developing since Triassic time, to begin an advance and to flourish greatly in the Cenozoic. The reptiles continued to dominate the scene and dinosaurs of great size and variety were numerous. They climaxed, however, and became extinct at the close of the period. Among the marine animals there were no great changes except that the ammonite cephalopods reached large sizes and developed very complex shells. However, they also became extinct at the close of the period.

The Cenozoic Era witnessed the development of most of the modern forms of life and it has been in this 60 million years that the earth has taken on its modern appearance. Of outstanding significance in this era was the disappearance of the dinosaurs, the flying reptiles, and the marine reptiles, and the appearance and wide expansion of the mammals. The development of the mammals would provide material for a book in itself, and will not be discussed in great detail here. A marvelous record of this development is preserved in the sediments of the Great Plains of the United States where much of the development took place.

The development of the mammals, most of which has taken place in the last million years, has been climaxed, so far as we are concerned, with the advent of man.

USES OF FOSSILS

Fossils are commonly used for four purposes.

1. A study of fossils tells us what the animals of the past were like and by studying the fossils of successively younger rocks we can more easily find out about, and understand, the changes which took place as different groups developed.

2. By studying fossils and comparing them with modern forms of life we can better understand the conditions under which the fossilized animals lived. By doing this we can then reconstruct the extent of ancient seaways, lakes, rivers, swamps, or other geographic features.

3. We commonly find that many rock formations contain the same fossils throughout their extent. If we know what fossils are characteristic of one formation, we can readily identify it at widely separated places, even on opposite sides of a mountain range. This use of fossils is very important if the formation being traced contains oil, or some valuable metal or other economic resource.

4. Another closely related use we make of fossils is comparing the ages of rocks in different parts of a continent or even on different continents. For example, certain rock layers in Russia, Germany, England, Timor, and Texas all contain very similar fossils, and we think therefore that they are of the same age. Also certain beds in Wyoming, along the south shore of Hudson Bay in Greenland, and in the Baffin Islands contain nearly identical fossils. Hence we have a means of correlating these beds and determining their relative age.

PRESERVATION OF FOSSILS

The fossil record generally consists of two types of material. One is that in which the organism itself, or some of its hard parts, is preserved without alteration. The other is the preservation of the organism or of its parts by alteration or modification to preservable material. The conditions most likely to allow a plant or animal to become a fossil are (1) possession of hard or durable parts, (2) quick burial which prevents the destruction of the organism.

Unaltered Remains

Many shells buried in the mud of the sea floor may continue to exist with little alteration for long periods of time, even after the mud surrounding them becomes hardened to form a rock. Many of our common fossils have been formed in this way.

Rare, but still occurring in considerable numbers, are the carcasses of large mammals of the Ice Age which have been found preserved in the frozen tundra of Siberia where they were probably entombed for as much as 25,000 years. In some cases on record the flesh of these animals has been so well preserved that it was fit to be eaten by the dogs of the exploration parties. The hard parts of many insects have been preserved by being encased in fossil resin (amber).

More common, but less spectacular, are the many thousands of bones of fossil mammals found in the sediments of the Great Plains areas, and the ancient fossil shellfish found in the sandstones and limy sediments of areas which were once marginal to the oceans. Typical of these are the fossil shells found in the rocks of Scott and Howard counties, Missouri.

Altered Remains

Most of the common fossils have been preserved as the result of alteration of the buried organism, especially its hard parts, to materials that are durable. This alteration may take any of several forms.

1. *Replacement:* Under certain conditions ground water may dissolve part or all of the original material and deposit in its place some other substance. In some cases the entire organism may be replaced and all its details of structure destroyed. In others, as often happens in fossil wood, the details of structure may be preserved in the minutest detail. The materials commonly replacing the original are calcite, silica, dolomite, and pyrite. Some pyrite fossils become altered to limonite.

2. *Permineralization:* Porous materials such as bones or porous shells are often altered by introduction of mineral substances into the pore spaces without otherwise altering the original material. In most cases the added mineral matter increases the weight of the preserved fragment and nearly always makes it more durable.

3. *Distillation:* The soft parts of living organisms contain certain amounts of nitrogen, oxygen, and hydrogen, in addition to the carbon. During fossilization all but the carbon may be removed leaving only a carbonaceous film preserved in the rocks. Many of these films show in excellent detail the structure of the organism. This type of preservation has formed many of our best plant fossils in the shales associated with coal beds.

4. *Impressions, molds, and casts:* Many fossils are formed by a shell or other hard part of an organism being impressed in soft mud and later removed leaving the impression to be preserved as a mold. In some cases shells such as snail and clam shells become filled with mud which hardens and when the shell is removed by solution or other means the filling remains as a mold showing the details of the inside of the shell. These are called internal molds. If the mold is of the external part of the shell, it is called an external mold. If either mold is later filled with some other substance forming a replica of the original, it is called a cast.

5. *Tracks, trails, and burrows:* As the animals of the past crawled about on the soft sediments of the ocean floor or walked about in the soft mud of swamp or stream bottom they left many footprints, tracks, and trails. Many of these are preserved as the mud or soft sediment is hardened to form rock.

In addition to these tracks and trails of the burrowing animals there are many cases of preservation of burrows or tubes formed by worms in the mud.

6. *Pseudofossils:* Many objects formed by natural processes have the appearance of being organic. Many of these are very much like true

fossils in appearance and are often mistaken for fossils. They are called pseudofossils or false fossils. Among the most common of these are concretions and nodules which assume many fantastic shapes and are very intriguing. All of the so-called "petrified eggs, potatoes, cantaloupes, oranges, and turtles" in the Missouri Ozarks are concretions or nodules (See Plate 17). The so-called fossil lizards are most frequently preserved mud cracks. The large "fossil bones or skeletons" are usually grotesque nodules or erosional forms that have assumed such shapes.

WHERE TO LOOK FOR FOSSILS

Fossils occur only in rocks which originated under conditions suitable to the life of an organism and to its preservation after death. They do not occur in igneous rocks such as granite, lava, or porphyry that have been formed from molten masses. Neither are they abundant in rocks which have undergone considerable change or metamorphism, because even though they may have been in the original rock, the forces of heat, pressure, and solution have altered the rock and destroyed the fossils.

Fossils are found in greatest abundance in those sediments which accumulate on the ocean floor between low tide and depths of 600 feet. The sedimentary rocks most commonly formed there are limestone and limy shale. Some sandstones contain considerable quantities of fossil remains; this is particularly true of sandstones which were deposited in river flood plains or in swampy areas where both plant and animal life were abundant.

The best places to look for fossils are where these types of rock are accessible. Some of the most productive localities in Missouri are rocky slopes and ledges which have been exposed to weathering. Quarries and road cuts generally provide good collecting, especially from the blocks that have been left exposed to the weather for some time. Some formations yield fossils readily while the rock is fresh, but some need a period of weathering before the fossils become loosened. The spoil piles of coal strip mines commonly contain many fossils.

A few of the good fossil localities in Missouri, are here listed by the rock formations of the geologic age in which they are found.

Tertiary—Some of the old clay pits in Stoddard County contain well-preserved fossil leaves.

Cretaceous—The Cretaceous beds in Missouri are sparsely fossiliferous and there are no good collecting localities in beds of this age.

Pennsylvanian—Spoil piles of strip mines in west central Missouri yield many good fossils. The dark shales associated with the coal beds often contain many well preserved plant fossils. The fire clay pits, and the clay layer under the coal beds have also yielded many fossilized tree trunks and stumps. Limestone quarries in the Kansas City area have produced many good fossils, especially from the shaly layers.

Mississippian—Many fossils occur in the quarries in the Burlington limestone from the central part of the state, southwestward toward Springfield and Carthage. Actually better than the quarries are weathered slabs on hillsides in this same formation. King's Butte, north of Springfield, has been a favorite hunting spot for lower Mississippian fossils for many years. The old Sweeney Quarry near Clifton City in Cooper County has yielded many excellent fossils.

Devonian—Some of the best Devonian fossils have come from exposures of rock along Little Saline Creek in Ste. Genevieve County. Other good ones may be found in creek valleys and rock quarries in southern Callaway and Boone counties and in western Montgomery County. One particularly good locality is in the Snyder Creek shale along the north side of a gravel road about 2 miles east of New Bloomfield.

Silurian—The Silurian beds of Missouri are rather limited in thickness and areal extent and do not contain fossils in great abundance. However, a few localities in the vicinity of Cape Girardeau and Bowling Green have yielded Silurian fossils in limited numbers.

Ordovician—Some of the Ordovician beds contain abundant fossils and others do not. In the Ozark Region fossils are most commonly found in the chert residue which appears after the dolomite and limestone formations are weathered. Few fossils are found in place in the dolomites. Diligent search of the chert in the hills of the Ozark Region will produce large numbers of gastropods and brachiopods, and a few trilobites and cephalopods.

The Kimmswick limestone at Glen Park, Jefferson County, as well as at other exposures in eastern Missouri has yielded large numbers of fossils. This is the only formation in Missouri which contains the "Sunflower Coral."

The Plattin formation contains many fossils at some localities. Among the better collecting localities are the highway and railroad cuts in the vicinity of Eureka, St. Louis County, and Herculaneum, Jefferson County; and the road cut just north of New London near the Salt River bridge in Ralls County. The shaly beds there contain large numbers of conodonts.

Cambrian—Fossils are not very abundant in the Cambrian beds of Missouri. In a few localities in the vicinity of Ironton the Bonne Terre formation contains small phosphatic brachiopods. Also the Davis formation in a few places contains brachiopods and rarely a trilobite.

THE ETHICS OF COLLECTING

If the collector should happen to make a rare or unusual find, he should protect it until it can be examined by some well-informed person. Many valuable fossils have been destroyed or lost because of improper care through ignorance or indifference and a good collector will do his best to see that such things do not happen.

In case of such an unusual find the collector should notify the paleontologist at some university or college geology department or at the Missouri Geological Survey. The Geology Department at the University of Missouri, Columbia, will be glad to receive notice of any unusual find, and to help the collector identify his material.

Fossil collectors, like other hobbyists, should obey the rules of good sportsmanship. This means respecting the rights of others and refraining from vandalism or destruction of other people's property. Many good fossil localities are on private property, and the rights of the owners should be respected and permission obtained before entering the property. Fossil sites on public land should be treated carefully so as to preserve their value to other collectors.

EQUIPMENT FOR COLLECTING

Fossil collecting is an inexpensive hobby because it requires only a minimum of equipment. It is helpful to have a hammer and a carrying bag of some sort and it is also advantageous to have one or two chisels, a magnifying lens, paper labels, and a notebook.

Almost any kind of hammer can be used, but the most satisfactory type is that known as a prospector's pick. A bricklayer's or mason's hammer is also satisfactory.

The collecting bag need not be elaborate but should be made of durable material. One of the most satisfactory readymade bags is the army musette bag.

The magnifying lens, while not essential, is very helpful in studying the finer details of many kinds of fossils. Lenses vary in price from less than a dollar to as much as twelve dollars. A lens of about 10-power magnification is most satisfactory for general use.

For final cleaning of the fossils a stiff-bristle brush and a needle holder with assorted sizes of needles are very helpful.

Another important item of equipment for the serious collector is a set of county highway maps, or a set of topographic maps. On these maps he can mark the collecting localities for his own future reference, or for the future use of other collectors.

PREPARATION OF SPECIMENS

The collector will soon realize that the fossils seen in museums were not found in such fine condition in the field but have undergone considerable preparation. The most important part of the preparation is the removal of the matrix or surrounding material. It is usually better to leave this part of the work to be done when time and care can be used. The average invertebrate fossils will not require much attention beyond the uncovering. Those which are composed of marcasite (a brassy yellow mineral) should be coated with shellac or collodion to prevent decomposition of the mineral and destruction of the fossil. Some of the more fragile specimens can be protected by saturation with shellac or thinned collodion, either of which will serve to stiffen or harden the specimen.

Bone fragments are likely to slake and crumble when they are exposed to the air and as the matrix is removed from such fossils they should be coated with shellac or some other protective coating.

Conodonts, ostracodes, and other micro-fossils are most commonly recovered from shales or shaly limestones and this is best accomplished by boiling the sample in water. The mud can generally be removed by occasionally pouring off the muddy water and replacing with clear water. Some samples will clean more easily if boiled in water to which small amounts of washing soda are added. If the shales are limy and the lime prevents them from breaking down easily, a small amount of dilute acetic acid may be helpful. This will dissolve the calcareous fossils but will not affect phosphatic ones such as conodonts and fish teeth. After the rock is broken down by boiling, and the mud washed away, the micro-fossils can be picked out with the moistened tip of a fine camel's hair brush. They can then be kept in small bottles or mounted in small cardboard slides. This type of work involves the use of a microscope and is therefore not so likely to be followed by the average collector.

A few limestones contain fossils which have been replaced by silica and these are best removed by dissolving the rock in diluted commercial hydrochloric acid (muriatic acid) which does not attack the silicified fossils. This process should be used with extreme caution. The acid should be placed only in glass or pottery containers, and should not be allowed to come in contact with the skin or clothing. It will eat holes in cotton cloth very rapidly. The fumes from this acid are corrosive and will cause metal objects to rust or corrode. Great caution is required in its use.

LABELING AND CATALOGING COLLECTIONS

If a fossil is to have scientific value, and be useful in geological work, it is necessary to keep a record of the locality and formation from which it came. It is a simple matter to record this information on small paper labels which should then be kept with the specimen. It has been said that "the label without the specimen is more valuable than the

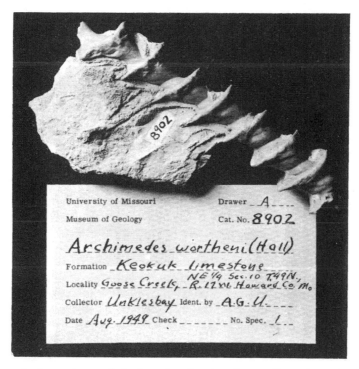

Figure 4. A specimen of *Archimedes* showing the small patch of white enamel with number on it, and the label pertaining to the specimen.

specimen without the label." Small cardboard trays make very convenient containers for the label and the specimen.

For the collector who is interested in doing a thorough job of collecting and arranging his material in orderly fashion, it is advisable to keep a catalog. To do this a number should be applied to each specimen (or group of specimens of the same species) from each locality and this number should also be marked on the label, and entered in the catalog or record book opposite the information pertaining to the entry. A very satisfactory way of applying the number is to paint a small patch of light colored enamel or lacquer on the specimen and then put the number on this with black drawing ink. Clear shellac will help to preserve such a number. (See Figure 4). After this is done, the specimen will not lose its identity if it becomes separated from its label.

Where to Get Help

There may be many times when the collector will have difficulty in identifying some of his fossils, or in being certain as to the identity of the formation in which he found them. In such cases he can get help from the paleontologists at any of the colleges or universities in the state, or from the Missouri Geological Survey. Many of these places will have displays or museum specimens which can be studied. The identity of the rock formation from which a fossil came is a very important part of the value of the fossil.

There are textbooks and manuals of paleontology and these can be consulted in many libraries. Also encyclopedias contain sections devoted to fossils of various kinds. This Handbook contains a list of useful reference books which the interested collector may buy or consult in libraries.

CLASSIFICATION OF FOSSILS

To make the study of animals and fossils easier and more meaningful we need to have some method of grouping related forms together. We call this a classification or taxonomic scheme. In doing this the student of fossils follows essentially the same scheme used by the biologist except that some biologic groups are not well represented as fossils and not so important to the paleontologist. Also the paleontologic classification is by necessity based on the preserved hard parts and therefore should be expected to differ slightly from the biological one which is based largely on the soft parts of the organism.

The world of living things is divided into two Kingdoms, Plant and Animal. These Kingdoms are divided into Phlya, which are further divided into Classes, Orders, Families, Genera, and Species, in decreasing order of importance. In some cases specialized intermediate groups are used. An illustration of the taxonomic scheme is the classification of the common cat, *Felis domestica*:

Kingdom — Animalia
    Phylum — Vertebrata
        Class — Mammalia
            Order — Carnivora
                Family — Felidae
                    Genus — *Felis*
                        Species — *domestica*

For purposes of international uniformity the generic and specific names are always Latinized and are published in Roman letters.

The paleontologist commonly recognizes 13 phyla of the Animal Kingdom:

1. Protozoa—One-celled organisms (shell bearing forms preserved as fossils)
2. Porifera—The sponges (fossil record poor)
3. Coelenterata—Hydroids and corals (corals abundant as fossils)
4. Platyhelminthes—Flatworms (not known as fossils)
5. Nemathelminthes—Threadworms (not known as fossils)
6. Trochelminthes—Wheelworms (not known as fossils)
7. Annelida—Segmented or annulated worms (fossil record poor)
8. Echinodermata—Starfish, sea lilies, sea urchins (abundant as fossils)
9. Bryozoa—The moss-like animals (abundant as fossils)
10. Brachiopoda—The lamp shells (abundant as fossils)
11. Mollusca—Clams, oysters, snails, etc. (abundant as fossils)
12. Arthropoda—Crabs, lobsters, crayfish, insects, spiders, etc. (abundant as fossils)
13. Vertebrata—Animals with backbones—fish, amphibians, reptiles, birds, mammals (abundant as fossils)

This handbook begins with the Protozoa and proceeds through the more complex groups in order, with particular emphasis on those that are common in Missouri rocks.

PHYLUM PROTOZOA

This phylum includes the simplest and most primitive animals. They consist of a single cell of protoplasm which by itself performs all the functions of living—feeding, digestion of food, excretion of waste matter, breathing, locomotion, growth, and reproduction. Many protozoa are without a skeleton, but some form small shells of calcareous or siliceous material. They are mostly small in size, ranging from the size of fine sand grains to a few forms which reach as much as 2 inches or more in diameter.

The shell-bearing forms are common as fossils. These are the Radiolaria and the Foraminifera. The Radiolaria secrete very beautiful skeletal-like shells of silica which are amazingly intricate and delicate. They do not, however, occur in abundance in the rocks of Missouri.

The Foraminifera are mostly marine, and form shells of limy material or of sand grains cemented together by a sticky substance secreted by the animal. This group of animals includes a great number of genera which secrete shells of greatly diverse size and shape. They are known in the rock column from Ordovician to Recent and are very abundant in modern oceanic and fresh waters.

The only group of the Protozoa that is abundant as fossils in Missouri is that group known as the fusulinids. These were small animals

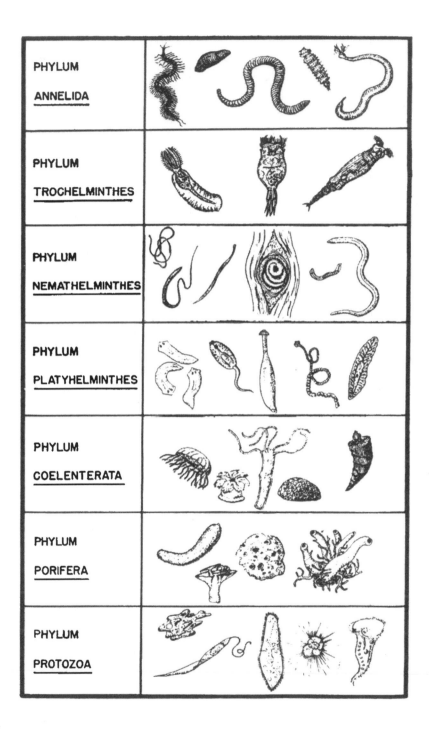

PHYLUM ANNELIDA	
PHYLUM TROCHELMINTHES	
PHYLUM NEMATHELMINTHES	
PHYLUM PLATYHELMINTHES	
PHYLUM COELENTERATA	
PHYLUM PORIFERA	
PHYLUM PROTOZOA	

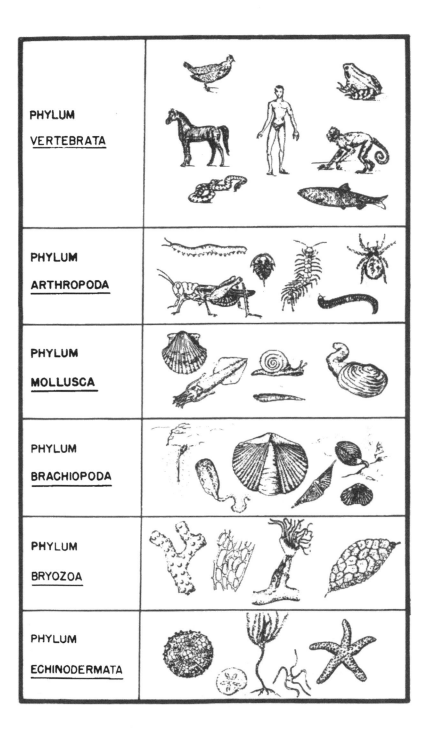

PHYLUM VERTEBRATA	
PHYLUM ARTHROPODA	
PHYLUM MOLLUSCA	
PHYLUM BRACHIOPODA	
PHYLUM BRYOZOA	
PHYLUM ECHINODERMATA	

which secreted a shell about the size and shape of a grain of wheat and they are often called "petrified wheat grains." These forms occur as fossils in the Pennsylvanian limestones and limy shales where they are fairly abundant in some localities. Detailed study of the fusulinids is made by making thin sections which show the internal structure of the shell. The external appearance and internal structure of the shells is shown in Plate 1, Figs. 2, 4, 5.

In some Mississippian limestones there are large numbers of somewhat similar but more primitive forms called endothyroids.

It should be pointed out that the small size of the protozoans makes them difficult to study, and it is impossible to do much with them without a microscope. Therefore they are not usually of much interest to the average amateur. However the very fact that they are minute and difficult to handle makes them a fascinating challenge, and to the amateur who has access to a microscope they provide material for an interesting hobby.

PHYLUM PORIFERA

This phylum includes the forms commonly called sponges. They are the earliest and most primitive of the many-celled animals and represent an advance over the Protozoa in that certain cells perform certain of the functions necessary for growth and reproduction. Most of the sponges are marine, but a few types are common in fresh-water ponds and lakes.

Structurally the sponge consists of a central cavity surrounded by a porous wall. This wall consists of fleshy layers supported and stiffened by a network of spicules. The spicules may be composed of silica, calcium carbonate, or a leathery substance known as spongin.

The fossil record of the sponges consists mainly of spicules preserved in fine-grained sediments, but a few forms are known which seem to represent molds and casts of the entire sponge. Sponges are known from pre-Cambrian to present time but are not abundant in the rocks of Missouri.

Some sponge spicules occur in the Ordovician Jefferson City formation and in a few other formations but they are not easily recognized. (See Plate 1. Fig. 7.)

QUESTIONABLE SPONGES

Receptaculites—This genus, commonly called the "Sunflower Coral," is abundantly represented in the Ordovician Kimmswick limestone of eastern Missouri. The specimens are often referred to as "petrified sunflowers," and Figure 6 on Plate 1 illustrates the reason for this name.

From all appearances this genus seems to belong with the sponges but it does not fit well into any established subdivision of this phylum. It is considered by some workers to be closely related to the corals.

Receptaculites is a very distinctive form that is easily recognized and serves very well in identifying the Kimmswick formation. It also occurs in Ordovician rocks of other states.

PHYLUM COELENTERATA

The coelenterates are primitive animals which are only slightly advanced over the Porifera. They constitute a large group which has existed in aquatic environments at least since Cambrian time, and they have left one of the most complete of fossil records. Their abundance and good preservation as fossils have allowed extensive study of their record and their abundance in modern waters has led to a fairly satisfactory understanding of the characteristics of the group in general.

Four classes of this phylum are represented in the fossil record and these are: (1) Class Hydrozoa, (2) Class Stromatoporoidea, (3) Class Scyphozoa, (4) Class Anthozoa.

Class Hydrozoa

This class includes the common fresh-water *Hydra* and the more complex small marine jellyfishes. Although they are not unusual in the fossil record of many areas, they have not been reported in Missouri.

Class Stromatoporoidea

This class contains an assortment of extinct marine forms whose taxonomic position is somewhat uncertain. They are somewhat coral-like, but also bear some resemblance to the sponges and even to algae. They secrete a calcareous skeleton which may occur in various shapes but are commonly dome-shaped or rod-like masses of thin cellular layers.

The Stromatoporoids have been important rock builders in the past and are known in the geologic record of Ordovician, Silurian, and Devonian rocks.

In Missouri they occur abundantly in the Devonian limestones and are commonly associated with beds containing numerous corals (See Fig. 1, Plate 1).

Class Scyphozoa

This class includes the jellyfishes, which, because they lack hard parts, are very unusual as fossils. A few exceptional specimens have been found as impressions in shales and they range as far back as the Cambrian. None has been reported from Missouri.

Class Anthozoa

This class includes a group of marine animals which live attached to rocks or other shells in the sea. They have more complicated internal cavities than have the other members of the phylum, and these cavities are divided by partitions called mesenteries. The presence of the mesenteries in the soft part of the animal is reflected in the skeleton by the formation of vertical partitions called septa. The Anthozoa are commonly known as the "flower animals" because the ring of tentacles surrounding the mouth resembles the petals of a flower. Many of the forms are brilliantly colored in life, and a group of them growing together on the sea floor truly resembles a flower garden.

Two types of Anthozoa occur. The soft-bodied forms without a skeleton are called sea anemones and the forms which secrete a rigid external skeleton are called corals. The skeleton is most commonly of calcareous material. The anemones have left no fossil record but the corals are both abundant as fossils and in modern seas. They are particularly abundant in warm clear seas, where they commonly form large reefs. The Great Barrier Reef of Australia, and the coral islands of the Pacific are typical examples.

Some corals grow alone and form an individual skeleton for each animal. They are called "solitary" forms. Others grow closely packed together in a colony in which they develop common supporting structures used by more than one individual. These are said to be "colonial" or "compound," and the skeletal mass formed by the colony is called a corallum.

Corals are commonly divided by the paleontologist into four groups, based primarily on the arrangement of the septa, but other factors are also used for making finer distinctions.

1. The Tetracoralla—An extinct group of exclusively Paleozoic corals in which the septa are arranged in cycles of four. They may be colonial or solitary. Solitary forms are commonly called "horn corals."

2. The Hexacoralla—A group in which the septa are arranged in cycles of six. They are the dominant corals in modern seas and are known in the fossil record since Mesozoic time. They may be colonial or solitary.

3. The Octocoralla, also called Alcyonaria—A group in which there are eight septa in the skeleton and eight tentacles in the soft part of the body. This group is known to have lived as early as Ordovician time and some members still exist in modern seas. Among the modern ones are the "Sea Fans" of the genus *Gorgonia*. The Octocoralla are mostly colonial.

4. The Tabulata—A group in which the septa are absent or poorly developed but in which there commonly exist horizontal partitions called *tabulae*. This group is now extinct but is known in the fossil

record of the Paleozoic and Mesozoic. They are invariably colonial and the coralla are of many shapes and sizes. This group was fairly abundant from Ordovician to Pennsylvanian and a few forms persisted to the end of the Mesozoic. They were important reef builders during the Paleozoic and are abundant as fossils (See Plates 2 and 3).

Of these four groups of corals only the Tetracorals and the Tabulata are common in Missouri. Typical common representatives, listed below, are illustrated in Plates 2, 3, and 4.

Tetracorals
    Pennsylvanian
        Lophophyllidium
    Mississippian
        Amplexus
        Zaphrentis
        Lithostrotionella
    Devonian
        Hexagonaria
        Streptelasma
        Zaphrentis
        Cyathophyllum
        Cystiphyllum
        Amplexus
        Heliophyllum
    Silurian
        Zaphrentis
    Ordovician
        Tetradium
        Streptelasma
        Favistella
Tabulata
    Pennsylvanian
        Chaetetes—sometimes called the "hair coral"
    Mississippian
        Auloporidae—sometimes called the "creeping coral"
    Devonian
        Favosites—sometimes called "petrified honey combs"
    Silurian
        Favosites
        Halysites—sometimes called the "Chain Coral"
    Ordovician
        Chaetetes

PHYLUM BRYOZOA

The animals of this group are called Bryozoa or "moss animals" because living colonies bear close resemblance to growing moss. The individual animals are microscopic in size but each possesses the organs to perform all the functions of living. They live in water, mostly marine, and they build colonial skeletons of chitinous or calcareous material.

Bryozoa are abundant and very widespread in present oceans and in some fresh water. They prefer clear, well-circulated water. They have been abundant since early Ordovician time and are fairly common as fossils. More than 1500 species are known from Paleozoic rocks.

Because of the microscopic nature of the individuals and the complexity of the colonial arrangements, the Bryozoa have not been studied by many paleontologists. However, the small size of the individuals and the fact that small fragments of a colony are identifiable make them valuable and important fossils.

Bryozoa are common in several Missouri formations and in general they can be classed in four common types. These are (1) the branching types, (2) the fenestellate or "lacy" types, (3) the *Archimedes* types, and (4) the "starfish" type.

The branching forms occur most commonly in beds of Ordovician age, especially in the Kimmswick and Plattin limestones, but are also common in Pennsylvanian beds (see Plates 2 and 14).

The fenestellate or lacy forms began in Silurian time, were very abundant in Mississippian, and continued into the Pennsylvanian. They are typified by the genus *Fenestella* which in fossil form resembles bits of lace impressed in the rock (Fig. 7 on Plate 3).

The *Archimedes* type of Bryozoa is sometimes called the "fossil corkscrew." This form consists of a spiral screw-like body of calcium carbonate. During life this spiral formed the core or central axis of a colony of fenestellate bryozoan which was attached to and wrapped loosely around the core with the lacy "fronds" extending outward. Some of the cores are found with fragments of the fronds attached but it is not certainly known that all fenestellate forms had such an axis. The name is derived from the similarity of this spiral to the "Archimedes screw" invented by the great philosopher Archimedes to lift water from lower to higher levels. They are fairly common in Missouri in the Mississippian Keokuk and Chester limestones and are known to range upward into the Pennsylvanian in some areas (See Fig. 4, and Plate 3).

The "starfish" type of Bryozoa is more correctly called *Evactinopora* but receives its common name from the fact that it is star-like in shape. This form occurs in the middle and upper part of the Mississippian. They are abundant in the Fern Glen of St. Louis County and the St. Joe and Reed's Spring formation of southwestern Missouri (See Plate 2, Fig. 9).

WORMS

Early workers in zoology and in paleontology recognized a phylum called Vermes which included the worm and worm-like creatures. Closer study revealed rather significant differences among these forms and they are now recognized as forming four phyla.

1. Platyhelminthes (flatworms)
2. Nemathelminthes (threadworms)
3. Trochelminthes (wheel worms)
4. Annelida or Annulata (annulated worms)

PHYLUM PLATYHELMINTHES

This group includes the "flatworms" which are unsegmented and almost always without an anal opening. They are dominantly parasitic in living habit. One of the commonly known forms is the liver fluke which is parasitic in sheep.

There are no undoubted fossil remains of this group.

PHYLUM NEMATHELMINTHES

This group is composed of the common round worms or thread worms of which a common form known to most people is the black "horsehair worm." Some of these forms are parasitic and quite dangerous to the host. An example is the *Trichina* or "pork worm."

Fossil evidence of these worms occurs in rocks as old as Cambrian but none is known from Missouri.

PHYLUM TROCHELMINTHES

The animals included in this group are those commonly called the "wheel animalcules" or "rotifers" which are abundant in stagnant pools of water. They are called rotifers because the constant vibration of small circlets of bristles near their heads causes the animal to appear to be in constant rotation in the water.

The Trochelminthes are of great interest because many corals, echinoderms, bryozoans, and brachiopods pass through an infant growth stage which closely resembles a mature Trochelminthe. This is called a trochophore larval stage and is thought by some to indicate that these forms developed out of earlier Trochelminthe ancestors.

Trochelminthes are not known as fossils.

PHYLUM ANNELIDA
(Annulata)

This phylum includes the animals that are most commonly thought of as worms. Basically they resemble a slender cylindrical tube with a mouth at one end and an anal opening at the other, and they are divided into a number of rings or segments. Probably the best known member of this phylum is the common earthworm.

The Annelida have had a long geologic history and are known as fossils from as early as Cambrian. It is not unlikely that many of the tubes and borings in pre-Cambrian rocks were formed by members of this phylum.

The fossil record of the worms consists of different types of evidence:

1. Burrows, borings, trails.
2. Impressions of soft bodies in mud.
3. Preserved chitinous jaws.
4. Preserved excremental pellets.
5. Calcareous tubes in which the worm lived.

Although not abundant in Missouri, evidences of ancient worms are present in some formations as illustrated in Plate 13. Portions of some rocks are referred to as "vermicular" because of the large number of worm tubes and borings. The Hannibal and Northview formations (Mississippian age) have been called the "Vermicular formation" because of the abundance of these borings.

PHYLUM BRACHIOPODA

The phylum Brachiopoda consists of a group of shell-bearing marine invertebrates which have existed since early Cambrian time and were very abundant throughout most of the Paleozoic. They form the most important group of Paleozoic fossils and are probably the most common fossils in Missouri. Many species are easy to recognize and are widespread so that they are very useful in making correlations between rock formations.

The shell of the brachiopod consists of two parts (valves) which are hinged so they can be opened or closed by the muscle system of the animal. The valves are unequal in size but each valve may be divided into two equal halves by a line through the mid-length of the valves. One of the valves is usually more convex than the other and it usually has an opening in its beak through which extends a stalk (pedicle) for attachment. This valve is called the pedicle valve (sometimes called the ventral valve). The other valve is called the dorsal or brachial valve and it encloses the animal's feeding organs. One of the common modern forms has somewhat the appearance of a Grecian oil lamp and the shells are commonly called "lamp shells."

The feeding and breathing organ of the brachiopod is a very distinctive characteristic and helps to distinguish the brachiopods from other invertebrates. This organ, called the lophophore or feeding organ consists of a pair of arms or brachia, one on each side of the mouth, extending away from the hinge side of the shell. In simplest form these are simple loops or fleshy tentacles supported by a calcareous core. In some of the more complicated forms the brachia are coiled into spirals which may be unwound during feeding and extended beyond the edge of the shell. The spiral supports for these coiled forms are sometimes preserved in the fossils and are used as a basis for classification (See Plate 9, Fig. 3).

The individuals may vary greatly in size. Some are only a fraction of an inch in length and others reach as much as 11 inches across the hinge. Many forms are known which are from 2 to 4 inches across the hinge.

In mature life the brachiopods are attached by the pedicle and they frequently grow in groups attached to rocks, pilings, or other objects in the sea water. Ordinarily they prefer shallow well-circulated water of normal salinity. There are, however, a few forms which prefer to live in a muddy environment and can stand water that is below normal salinity. A common one of these is the genus *Lingula* which has existed since early Cambrian time with very little or no change.

The classification of the brachiopods has been altered and revised from time to time and is based on many features. However, for our purpose it will suffice to divide them into two classes, (1) Inarticulata and (2) Articulata. These classes have been recognized by most workers and are based upon the nature of the hinge.

Class Inarticulata

This class includes those forms in which the hinge is poorly developed and the pedicle emerges from between the valves instead of from an opening in one valve. The shells in most of the inarticulates is of phosphatic or chitinous material similar to a fingernail, and are small disc-like (orbiculoid) or tongue-shaped (linguloid) shells. They are rather primitive in nature but have persisted from early Cambrian to the present time. The common inarticulate forms in Missouri are the linguloids and orbiculoids. The linguloids include the genus *Lingula*, which ranges from the Cambrian to recent time, and *Lingulella* and *Obolus* which are common in Cambrian rocks. The orbiculoids are probably most abundant in the black shales of the Pennsylvanian but occur also in other shale formations.

Class Articulata

This class includes most of the brachiopods and they are the ones in which the two valves have a well-developed hinge and muscle system. Most of the articulate shells are of calcareous material and the' pedicle emerges through a specialized opening in the pedicle valve.

The articulates have been arranged in orders according to the nature of the pedicle opening, and these orders have each been subdivided into families on the basis of shell form and internal structure. Inasmuch as classification based on these characteristics is sometimes difficult and highly technical it will not be elaborated upon here. For our purpose we will refer to the common articulate brachiopods of Missouri by more common, well-known, but not inaccurate, group names.

1. Orthids. Subcircular, flatly bi-convex forms with fairly strong radial ornamentation.
2. Pentamerids. Mostly thickly rounded smooth forms with short hinge lines.
3. Strophomenids. Mostly square-shouldered, concave-convex forms with strong radial ornamentation.
4. Productids. Spine-bearing forms. In some the spines are along the hinge line, but in most forms they are scattered over the entire shell.
5. Spire-bearing forms.
     These forms are called the spire-bearers because the lophophore is spirally coiled. They can be divided into three groups as follows:
   1. Spiriferoids. Those in which the lophophore begins to coil directly from its base and then extends sideways so that it points toward the sides of the shell. Most of the spiriferoids have long hinge lines.
   2. Athyroids. Those in which the initial portion of the lophophore extends outward from its base and then is coiled backward a short distance before the spiral coiling begins. The athyroid spires are commonly lower and broader than those of the spiriferoids and the shells are nearly circular in outline. The hinge line is relatively short.
   3. Atrypoids. Those forms in which the spires may point inward toward the middle of the shell or toward the dorsal or ventral valve. Most atrypoids have short hinge lines and globular shells.
6. Terebratulids. These are forms in which the lophophore is supported by stiff limy loops. The shells are most commonly thick and rounded, have short hinge lines and usually have prominent beaks. In most forms the pedicle opening is in the beak. This group contains most of the living brachiopods.
7. Rhynchonellids. The shells of this group are mostly triangular to rounded in outline and have shells which are strongly wrinkled. The hinge line is short and the beak is pointed. Both valves are convex.

PHYLUM MOLLUSCA

The Phylum Mollusca includes the forms most commonly known as the "shell fish," and of these the better known ones are the clams, oysters, and snails.

The phylum includes marine, fresh-water, and land invertebrates.

Most of them possess an external skeleton in the form of a shell, but some do not. The phylum is divided into five classes.

Class 1. Amphineura—Sea mice, chitons.
Class 2. Pelecypoda—Bivalves, oysters, clams, mussels.
Class 3. Scaphopoda—Tusk shells.
Class 4. Gastropoda—Snails and slugs.
Class 5. Cephalopoda—Squids, cuttlefish, nautiloids, octopus.

Only three of these, the pelecypods, gastropods, and cephalopods are common fossils in Missouri and only these will be discussed in detail here.

Class Pelecypoda

This class is probably the best known for it includes the marine oysters, clams, and scallops, which are important sources of food; and

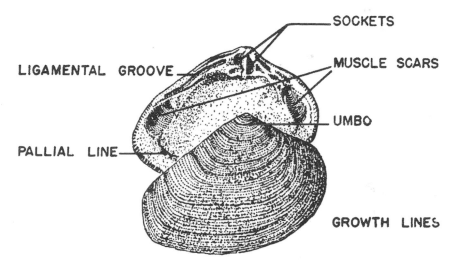

Figure 5. Sketch to show general characteristics of a pelecypod shell.

the fresh-water mussels whose shells are the chief source of material for making pearl buttons.

Typically the pelecypod consists of a slightly flattened fleshy mass which contains the animal's vital organs, and which possesses, on the outside, a set of gills for breathing. The forward portion of the body is composed of a modified "foot" which is a wedge-shaped muscular mass. This soft body is enclosed in a shell consisting of two parts called valves, and is attached to these valves by muscles which serve not only for attachment but also to open and close the shell (See Fig. 5).

In most pelecypods the valves are equal in size and are essentially mirror-images of each other. However in some forms, such as the oysters and scallops, the valves are not similar. The valves are hinged by a set of teeth and sockets and the nature of the hinge is important in classification. The shell is composed of three layers. The outermost layer is of chitin, a material somewhat similar to the human fingernail. It is usually thin in marine forms and thick in fresh-water forms. The middle layer is composed of calcium carbonate in closely packed prisms and is called the prismatic layer. The inner layer is also of calcium carbonate but is thinly layered and is pearly in appearance. This is called the "mother of pearl" layer and it is very well developed in fresh-water forms. In some genera the shells are smooth but many have ornamental ridges, spines, or nodes.

Pelecypods have existed since early Cambrian time. For the most part they have been inhabitants of the sea floor in shallow water (between the beach and 1200 feet depth). Some are capable of moving about but others live attached to rocks or pilings. More than 7000 species are known at present, and there is a great variety of shell forms.

The pelecypods range greatly in size. The largest is the *Tridacna* of the South Pacific which has shells as large as 5 feet in length, and the smallest ones are less than one-quarter inch in length.

Most of the fossil pelecypods in beds older than Pennsylvanian are preserved as molds and casts, but in the Pennsylvanian and younger beds many specimens occur in which the original shell material is preserved. When a pelecypod dies, its shell opens and is subject to being broken apart by waves and currents. Consequently fossil pelecypods commonly are represented by only one valve.

In Missouri, pelecypods are fairly common in beds of Ordovician (especially the upper Plattin and Kimmswick), Devonian, Mississippian, and Pennsylvanian ages. A common Missouri form is illustrated on Plate 13.

Class Gastropoda

This class includes forms commonly known as snails or slugs, and also the wide variety of variously shaped and colored marine forms commonly called "conchs." The gastropods are dominantly aquatic and live in both marine and fresh water, but they are also well represented by land-dwelling forms which live in damp shady places in woods and gardens.

This class contains a greater variety of forms than the other molluscan classes and over 20,000 species are known at present (See Figures 6 and 7). This great variety has not always been characteristic of the class, however, and the pre-Mesozoic forms were relatively simple and plain. The gastropods began to develop greater variety in the Mesozoic and continued to do so on into the Cenozoic. In fact it seems likely that they are now nearing the culmination of their development.

In most forms the soft body is enclosed in a univalved or single shell of calcium carbonate. This shell begins on the snail during its embryonic development as a small protoconch and grows with the animal. In most of the shell-bearing forms the shell is essentially a gradually expanding cone which is coiled about an axis (See Figure 6). A few forms do not

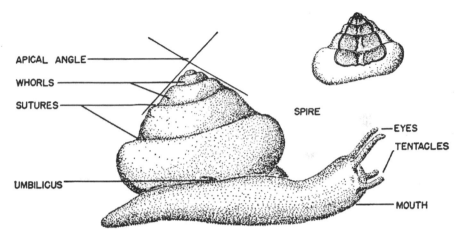

Figure 6. Simplified drawing of a common gastropod bearing a coiled shell. Inset sketch shows cutaway view to show method of coiling.

have coiled shells. The snail shell is unchambered and the animal, when retracted, occupies most of the shell. Some forms close the opening of the shell with a horny lid or operculum which is attached to the foot.

Most of the fossil gastropods of Missouri consist of internal or external molds of the shells but in many Pennsylvanian forms the shells have been preserved.

The zoological classification of the gastropods is based almost entirely on the soft part and this sort of classification is difficult for the paleontologist to use. For purposes of convenience we will group them into two groups: (1) the helical-spired forms in which the coiling is similar to that of a tapered cork-screw—some are high spired and others are low; (2) the plano-spiral forms in which the coiling is all in one plane and each coil encloses all previous ones.

Fossil gastropods are common in Missouri and some of them are shown in Plates 12 and 13.

Class Cephalopoda

The Class Cephalopoda is an exclusively marine group which includes the modern squid, cuttlefish, octopus, and the pearly nautilus. The

Figure 7. Sketches to show a few of the many varied forms assumed by gastropod shells.

class includes the most highly organized molluscs, and the largest of all living or fossil invertebrates. The giant squid of modern seas has tentacles as much as 35 feet in length, and the giant ammonites of the Cretaceous had coiled shells which were as large as 6 feet in diameter. In Ordovician seas there were giant forms with straight shells as much as 15 feet long and more than a foot in diameter.

In general the cephalopods are similar in structure to the other molluscs except that the forward part of the "foot" which surrounds the mouth is modified into a ring of tentacles. Also the eyes are highly developed and the mouth is provided with a pair of jaws and a rasping tongue. The gill cavity connects to the outside by means of a fleshy tube through which the animal may forcibly expel water to propel it backward through the water by "jet propulsion."

In most modern forms the shells are only rudimentary or lost entirely, but in the modern pearly nautilus the shell is like that of most fossil forms. The shell consists of only one valve which is essentially a coiled cone divided into chambers by transverse partitions called septa. Fossil forms have ranged from simple straight tapered cones with smooth saucer-like septa to tightly coiled forms with highly wrinkled septa. There is a great diversity among the fossil forms and this makes them very useful as index fossils.

This class is divided into three subclasses.

Subclass 1. Nautiloidea—Includes modern nautilus and fossil forms in which the septa are simple and have smooth edges. Range in age from Cambrian to Recent.

Subclass 2. Ammonoidea—An extinct group which had septa with strongly wrinkled edges. They were most abundant in the Mesozoic Era and are important index fossils for beds of that age. Range in age from Devonian to close of Cretaceous.

Subclass 3. Coleoidea—A group which contains the extinct belemnoid, and the squid, cuttlefish, and octopus. Not common as fossils.

Of these three subclasses the nautiloids and ammonoids are fairly common as fossils in Missouri.

The nautiloids of Missouri range in age from Ordovician to Pennsylvanian. Most of the Ordovician ones are large straight forms, some of which are several inches in diameter and a few feet in length. They are most common in the Kimmswick formation. The Jefferson City formation has yielded some closely coiled forms.

The Devonian beds have yielded moderate-sized straight and curved forms, but they are not very abundant. The Mississippian Chouteau limestone has yielded a considerable number of straight, curved, and coiled nautiloids but they are not greatly abundant.

The Pennsylvanian beds, particularly in the west central part of the state, have yielded a varied assortment of well-preserved coiled nautiloids and a few straight forms.

Some of the common Missouri nautiloids are illustrated in Plates 12 and 13.

The ammonoids are those forms in which the septa have wrinkled edges which are in contact with the shell wall. The pattern of these wrinkles is preserved in internal molds and is used in classification. The development of crenulations began in Devonian time and the patterns became more and more complex in Mississippian, Pennsylvanian, and Permian times, resulting in the formation of a large group of relatively small-sized cephalopods called goniatites and ceratites.

The ammonoids in Missouri occur in Devonian, Mississippian, and Pennsylvanian beds. They are fairly common in the latter two, but only one specimen is known from the Devonian. Some of the common Pennsylvanian forms are shown in Plate 16.

PHYLUM ARTHROPODA

The Phylum Arthropoda, whose name means "jointed foot," includes a large and varied group of invertebrates. They are highly developed forms with bodies that are segmented, bilaterally symmetrical, and have jointed appendages. This group includes such commonly known forms as the insects, crayfish, spiders, centipedes, and many other common forms. The size of the individual in this phylum ranges from the tiniest insect to the giant Japanese crab whose claws can span a distance of more than 10 feet.

The members of this phylum have invaded more different habitats than those of any other phylum and have been the most successful group in adaptation. They are common in the air, water, and soil, and in nearly all extremes of altitude and climatic variation. The phylum probably includes the greatest variety of all invertebrates. In the insects alone more than 500,000 species have been determined.

This phylum is divided into classes of which only the most common ones will be discussed here.

Class Crustacea—Crabs, crayfish, lobster, ostracodes and others.
Class Trilobita—Fossil trilobites.
Class Insecta—Flies, beetles, butterflies, and others.
Class Arachnida—Spiders, scorpions, eurypterids, and others.

Of these classes only the trilobites and crustaceans might be considered as common fossils in Missouri. Fossil insects and eurypterids have been reported but they are rare.

Class Crustacea

This class includes commonly known forms such as the crayfish, crabs, and lobsters. It also includes a common but lesser known group of small animals called ostracodes. The ostracodes are small (generally less than one-eighth of an inch) forms with a shell similar in appearance to a small clam shell, but in which one valve overlaps the edges of the other. They are common in fresh-water ponds and lakes, and inhabit some marginal marine and brackish water areas.

Fossil ostracodes occur in several formations in shaly layers associated with limestone. Because of the small size they are classed as microfossils. For the person who likes to work with microfossils and who has access to a microscope they are very interesting. They can usually be freed from the shale by soaking or boiling in water and flushing away the mud. Typical Missouri ostracodes are illustrated in Plate 16.

Class Trilobita

The trilobite is so-called because of the three-lobed development of its body which is divided into a middle lobe and two side lobes. Also the body is divided into three parts; (1) the pygidium or tail, (2) the thorax or abdomen, and (3) the cephalon or head. Most fossil trilobites consist of one of these parts and a complete individual is rather uncommon. The reason for this is that the trilobite moulted periodically. That is, it cast off its old shell from time to time and developed a new one. In moulting, the shell was lost a segment at a time, therefore each fossil trilobite does not represent a dead animal.

The trilobites of Missouri range widely in age and occur in all the Paleozoic systems in the state. They are not common in the Cambrian nor in the earlier Ordovician, but are fairly common in the later Ordovician Plattin and Kimmswick beds of east central Missouri. Silurian and Devonian trilobites are not abundant in the state but the Mississippian Chouteau beds have yielded quite a few. A few have also been found in the Burlington limestone. They are also fairly common in beds of Pennsylvanian age.

Some of the more common and characteristic trilobites from Missouri are illustrated in Plate 14.

PHYLUM ECHINODERMATA

This phylum contains a group of exclusively marine animals which have existed from Cambrian to modern times. It is well represented in modern seas by the starfish, sea urchins, sea cucumbers, feather stars, and sea lilies. In the fossil record the echinoderms are well represented and this phylum is an important one to the paleontologist.

Typically the soft parts of the echinoderm are contained in a skeleton consisting of calcareous plates held together by a leathery skin. The skeleton commonly is star-shaped but many are biscuit-like or egg-like in shape. All echinoderms develop with a basic pentameral (five-sided) symmetry. The skin is covered with spines.

The abundance of well-preserved fossils of this group has encouraged study and they are fairly well known. Some of the groups represented by fossils are now extinct.

This phylum is commonly divided into seven classes as follows:

Stemmed or attached	Class Cystoidea—extinct
	Class Edrioasteroidea—extinct
	Class Blastoidea—extinct
	Class Crinoidea—feather stars and sea lilies—living
Free to move	Class Stellaroidea (Asteroidea)—starfish—living
	Class Echinoidea—sea urchins and sand dollars—living
	Class Holothuroidea—sea cucumbers—living

Of these classes the Blastoidea and Crinoidea are common as fossils in Missouri and some specimens of Edrioasteroidea, Cystoidea, and Echinoidea are also known.

Class Cystoidea

This is the oldest group of stemmed or stalked echinoderms. They are so-called because of the cyst-like or bladder-like shape of the skeleton which is composed of calcareous plates of irregular shape, size, and arrangement. They range in age from Cambrian to late Paleozoic but most of them occur in Ordovician and Silurian rocks. They are not common in Missouri but a few have been found in the Kimmswick limestone.

Class Edrioasteroidea

This is a poorly understood class in which the individuals resemble a small rounded pillow or bun with a five-rayed star resting on the top. They are not common in Missouri.

Class Blastoidea

This is a class of extinct organisms which had small pear-shaped or globular skeletons at the end of a stalk. They resemble small flower buds. The skeleton is typically composed of 13 plates arranged in a radially symmetrical five-sided pattern. Five of the plates are forked and enclose a slotted area called the ambulacrum through which the feeding organs protrude.

Blastoids are fairly common in Missouri, particularly in the beds of Mississippian age and are frequently called "petrified acorns or hickory nuts." The common genera of these beds are *Pentremites* and *Cryptoblastus*. These are illustrated, along with other common genera in Fig. 10-15, Plate 5.

Class Crinoidea

This class includes the forms commonly called "sea lilies" or "feather stars." A normal crinoid consists of three principal parts, as shown in Figure 8. The most important part is the cup or calyx in which is contained the bulk of the animal's soft parts and vital organs. This calyx is composed of calcareous plates in symmetrical arrangement. The shape and arrangement of the plates are used to make generic classifications.

From the calyx the branching arms extend upward and outward to serve as food gatherers. The calyx is attached at its base to a stem or column which serves as a support. The column is composed of a number of disc-like segments or columnals which in life are held together by fleshy matter in such a way as to be flexible. Many stems are circular in cross-section but there are many variations and some are star-shaped. All of the discs have a central perforation so that the stem has a hollow tube extending through it. Upon the death of the animal the stem becomes broken into fragments consisting of one or more discs. These are commonly preserved in the rocks and are among the most common fossils. They are often mistaken for sections of the backbones of fish. They were collected and strung like beads by the early American Indians.

At the base of the stem there is a root or "holdfast" system which is formed by the branching of the stem somewhat like that of a tree-root system. Also there may be small branches along the stem. These are known as cirri and they are composed of plates similar to those of the stem.

The calyx or cup is the most important part of the fossil crinoid because upon it is based the generic and specific classification. Unfortunately the plates of the calyx commonly become dissociated after the animal dies and although they are not rare as fossils they are not as common as the stem fragments.

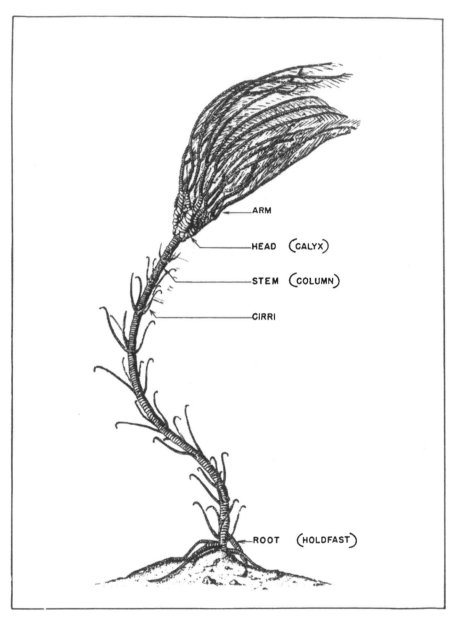

ARM

HEAD (CALYX)

STEM (COLUMN)

CIRRI

ROOT (HOLDFAST)

Figure 8. Sketch of a typical modern crinoid or "sea lily" showing the various parts.

Living crinoids occur chiefly in the Pacific and Indian oceans, and in the Caribbean .Sea. Locally they occur in great profusion, growing in large groups in clear warm water. There are as many as 650 known modern species.

Fossil crinoids also apparently grew in large groups because their distribution in the rocks is irregular. They occur in great numbers in some localities and formations and not at all in others. They have existed since Ordovician time.

Crinoids are quite abundant in Missouri, being known from Ordovician, Silurian, Devonian, Mississippian, and Pennsylvanian formations. Some beds of the Callaway limestone, and the Burlington limestone, are almost completely composed of crinoid remains. The Burlington is one of the best known crinoid-bearing formations in Missouri and throughout North America.

Typical crinoids from Missouri are illustrated in Plates 5 and 6.

Class Echinoidea

This class contains those forms now commonly known as sea urchins, sand dollars, and sea porcupines. They are forms in which the vital organs of the animal are enclosed within a globular to disc-like skeleton composed of calcareous plates. The outside of the skeleton bears large numbers of movable spines. All of these forms possess a five-rayed symmetry.

The echinoids are known to have existed from Ordovician to the present and to have been very abundant in the Mesozoic. They are not very common in Missouri but have been found in fairly large numbers in the St. Louis limestone.

The genus *Melonechinus* has been found in great numbers in the vicinity of St. Louis and specimens from the area have been sent to museums all over the world. One of the richest finds was made many years ago during excavations for one of St. Louis' large breweries. This genus is also sparsely scattered in other Mississippian beds in central Missouri (See Plate 7).

THE GRAPTOLITES

The fossils commonly called graptolites represent a group of extinct colonial marine animals that are only poorly understood. Many writers have placed them with the Coelenterata, but at present they are thought to belong with the hemichordates. They secreted a branching supporting skeleton of chitinous material in which the individuals lived in small pits along a slim stalk. They are commonly preserved as carbonaceous films on the bedding planes of dark shales. Here they resemble marks made with a pencil (hence the name, derived from the Greek *graptos* which means written.) In some cases they look very much like pieces of a small scroll saw blade impressed in the shale.

This group appeared in Ordovician time, reached a peak of numbers and variety in Silurian, and then dwindled to a few scattered remnants which continued into Mississippian time.

Graptolites are abundant and widespread in many areas, particularly in the black shales of the Ordovician in eastern United States. They are not really abundant in Missouri but some of the best preserved, uncrushed ones in this country occur in the Maquoketa (Ordovician) shales in Jefferson County (See Fig. 3 on Plate 1.). They also occur as poorly preserved carbonaceous films in the same formation in Pike County.

PHYLUM VERTEBRATA

This phylum contains all animals with a vertebral column or "backbone" and it is generally characterized by a highly organized nervous system. The members of this phylum can be divided readily into five groups: the fishes, the amphibians, the reptiles, the birds, and the mammals.

The earliest vertebrates of which we have a fossil record are fish-like forms of Ordovician age and the time since Ordovician has seen a great development in all groups. The fish have flourished continuously. The amphibians grew to large size and were fairly abundant in the Mississippian and Pennsylvanian times but have dwindled so that at present they are represented only by toads, frogs, and salamanders. The reptiles began development toward the end of the Paleozoic and reached tremendous size and numbers in Jurassic and Cretaceous. This group includes the widely publicized dinosaurs, some of which grew to lengths of 90 feet and weighed many tons—several times as much as a modern elephant. Birds seem to have developed from a group of reptiles that learned to fly and the oldest fossil that can be definitely called a bird is of Jurassic age. The mammals were later in developing. They began as archaic forms near the close of the Paleozoic but did not develop greatly until the Cenozoic Era.

Among the vertebrate fossils of Missouri, only the fish are commonly represented. Some mammals and reptiles have been found but they are not generally abundant, and amphibian remains are rare.

FISH

Fish are represented as fossils in Missouri by large numbers of teeth and tooth-like objects and by fossilized bony armor plates. These range

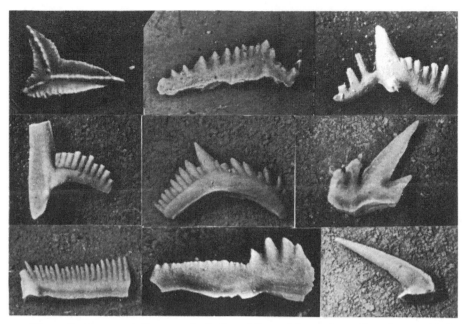

Figure 9. Representative conodonts from Missouri formations. Greatly magnified, approximately times 25. Photos by M. G. Mehl.

in age from Ordovician into Pennsylvanian and occur in abundance in some beds and localities. A few bone fragments have been found but they are not common.

One of the most common forms of teeth is from a shark-like creature called *Ptyctodus*. These teeth are not sharp-edged but are flattened plate-like forms. These "sharks" had their jaws "paved" with these flattened plates to facilitate the crushing of shell fish. The teeth are fairly common in portions of the Devonian limestones and shale, and in the basal Mississippian sandstone into which they have been reworked from Devonian beds.

The Burlington limestone also contains rather distinctive "shark" teeth which are larger and flatter than those of the Devonian beds. One of these is shown in Plate 13, Fig. 1.

Conodonts

Many beds in Missouri contain large numbers of small tooth-like objects called conodonts. These are probably the teeth of some fish-like organism. They occur in beds ranging from Ordovician to Pennsylvanian in age and are useful in making correlations between scattered exposures of the same bed. Because of their small size conodonts must be studied with a microscope. They can be recovered from the containing bed by boiling or crushing, if in shale, or if in limestone, using a solution of dilute acetic acid. The conodonts are not attacked by the acid. Representative Missouri conodonts are shown in Figure 9.

AMPHIBIANS

Amphibians did not appear until Devonian time but developed into large animals several feet in length by Pennsylvanian. After that, however, they dwindled until they are represented today only by frogs, toads, and salamanders. They are not common as fossils in Missouri. A few footprints of a supposed amphibian have been reported from Pennsylvanian shale near Kansas City, and a few frog bones were recovered from an old sinkhole near Enon, Moniteau County. The frog remains were of Pleistocene age.

REPTILES

Reptilian remains are scarce in Missouri. There have been a few reports of Cretaceous dinosaur fragments but these are indeed rare.

One of the more recent discoveries was made at Marble Hill in Bollinger County in 1942. Here, in beds of Cretaceous age, were found several dinosaur vertebrae. A few reptilian remains of Pleistocene age have been reported from a fissure in limestone near Herculaneum in Jefferson City, and turtles are known from an old sinkhole near Enon in Moniteau County. However, reptilian fossils are not abundant in Missouri.

MAMMALS

Fossil remains of mammals are not generally abundant in Missouri and can hardly be called common fossils, but many excellent finds have been made which always arouse a great deal of interest. Mammal fossils do not occur persistently in any one formation as do many of the invertebrates and their occurrences are isolated and unpredictable. Most mammal remains have been discovered in old caves and sinkholes and in the alluvial deposits along creeks and rivers.

Conspicuous among the mammalian remains that have been found are those of the mastodons, large elephant-like animals apparently present in large numbers. These are usually represented by skulls, teeth, ribs, and leg bones. It is believed that almost every county in the state has yielded at least one mastodon fragment. Also present, but in fewer numbers, are remains of the mammoth, close relative of the mastodons.

Several species of ancient horses are also known and fossil horse teeth are frequently discovered. Among the other mammals known as fossils in Missouri are the camel, deer, musk-ox, buffalo, bear, and peccary. In addition there is also some evidence for the existence of the raccoon, porcupine, and armadillo.

Figure 10. Large mastodon leg bone found in bed of Perche Creek, southwest of Columbia.

Not many localities have yielded mammalian remains in great numbers but a few of the outstanding ones are listed here:

A sinkhole near Enon in Moniteau County which contained many fragmental remains of horses and bones of a young mastodon, a tapir, and a sloth.

A cave beneath the old Lemp Brewery in St. Louis which yielded more than 3000 bones, most of which represented pig-like animals called peccaries, but also included a raccoon, a black bear, a porcupine, and an armadillo. These fossils are now in the American Museum of Natural History in New York.

A locality along Rock Creek about 20 miles south of St. Louis where, according to early literature, Dr. A. K. Koch collected a number of bones and teeth probably representing parts of several mastodons. Dr. Koch assembled these into an "animal" which he called *Missourium* and compared it with modern crocodiles and whales. He also compared it with the Leviathan described in the 41st Chapter of Job. His interpretation of these bones, along with some others he found in Gasconade County, aroused a very colorful controversy which was one of the most interesting events of the early history of geology in this country.

PLANT FOSSILS

The development of the plant kingdom has a long record which extends back to the fossilized masses of algae in pre-Cambrian rocks. Land plants did not develop until Silurian time, and even though they spread widely in Devonian and became very abundant and luxuriant in Pennsylvanian, plants did not become modernized until Cretaceous time.

The fossil record of plants in Missouri begins with algae-like masses in the Cambrian Bonne Terre dolomite. Silurian plants are not known in Missouri but the Devonian brown and black shales of northeastern Missouri contain unmistakable evidence of spore-bearing plants. In the vicinity of New London, Hannibal, and Louisiana these shales contain

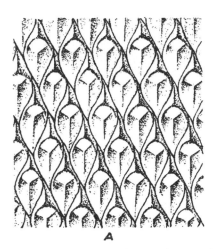 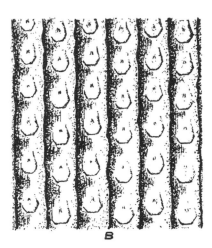

Figure 11. Sketches to show pattern left by scale-like leaves on Pennsylvanian scale-trees. A is *Lepidodendron* and B is *Sigillaria*.

small amber-colored, waxy-appearing disks which are the spores of plants. They are mostly microscopic in size but many are as large as small pin heads and can be seen without a microscope. Also present in some Devonian beds are molds, casts, and impressions of plant-like appearance and these may represent ancient "seaweeds."

In addition to these the Devonian, early Mississippian, and Pennsylvanian shales contain microscopic "fruits" of plants called chara. These are small, spherical, calcareous bodies with a spiral ornamentation.

The Pennsylvanian rocks contain large numbers of plant fossils which range from microscopic spores in the coal, to large tree trunks and stumps. The dark gray and brown shales which are associated with the coal beds commonly contain carbon-film impressions which closely

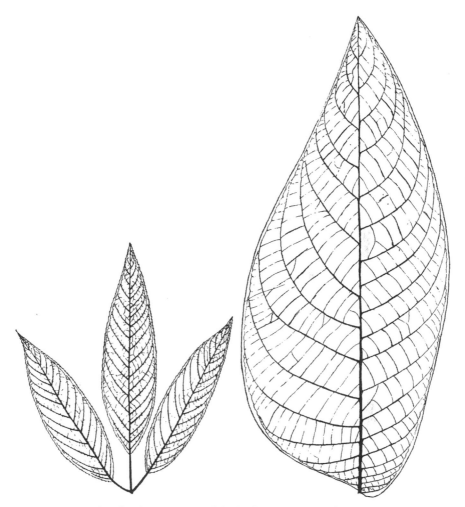

Figure 12. Sketch of reconstructed leaf of an Eocene walnut tree such as grew in southeastern Missouri.

Figure 13. Sketch of a reconstructed hickory leaf such as grew in southeastern Missouri during Eocene time.

resemble modern reeds, rushes, and ferns. Also in these beds, and commonly in the clay beneath the coal, there can be found large coalized fragments of "tree" trunks, roots, and branches. Several stumps have been found which are three to four feet across. These fossils are not from "trees" as we commonly think of trees today, but they are from large tree-like ferns and "scale trees." The scale trees were primitive plants in which scale-like leaves grew directly from the trunk and large branches, and there were no small branches or twigs. In one of these, called

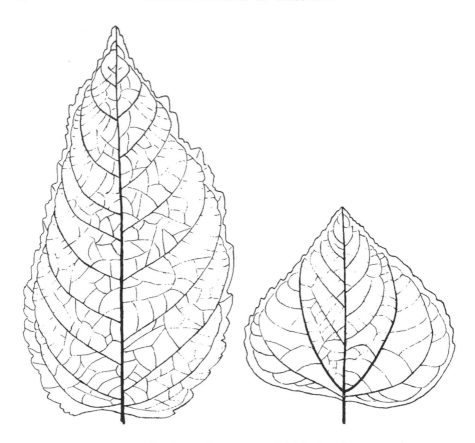

Figures 14 and 15. Sketches of reconstructed linden leaves such as grew in southeastern Missouri during Eocene time.

Lepidodendron, the leaves were in diagonal rows and in another called *Sigillaria* they were in vertical, parallel rows (See Plate 15 and Figure 11). Fossils of both of these, and particularly *Lepidodendron*, appear similar to the scale pattern of many reptiles and because of this they are often thought to be large "fossil snakes." The widespread coal beds of Missouri are composed largely of the remains of luxuriant swamp vegetation of Pennsylvanian time.

The Eocene beds in southeastern Missouri, particularly in Stoddard and Scott counties, contain many fossil plant leaves which are from plants closely related to, and closely resembling modern plants. Represented by fossil leaves are such modern trees as the walnut, hickory, linden, and sycamore. Drawings of leaves typical of these fossils are presented in Figures 12, 13, 14, and 15.

SUGGESTED REFERENCES

The following books are listed as sources of additional and more detailed information concerning fossils.

General Works

BEERBOWER, JAMES R. *Search for the Past: An Introduction to Paleontology.* Prentice-Hall, Inc., 1960.

BROUWER, A. *General Palaeontology.* University of Chicago Press, 1967.

FENTON, C. L. *Life Long Ago.* New York: Reynol & Hitchcock, 1937.

GOLDRING, WINIFRED. *Handbook of Paleontology for Beginners and Amateurs.* Albany: New York State Museum, 1929.

KUMMEL, BERNHARD, AND RAUP, DAVID. *Handbook of Paleontological Techniques.* W. H. Freeman & Co., 1965.

MATTHEWS, WM. H., III. *Fossils: An Introduction to Prehistoric Life.* Barnes & Noble, 1962.

SIMPSON, G. G. *Life of the Past.* New Haven: Yale University Press, 1953.

Invertebrates

MOORE, R. C., LALICKER, C. G. AND FISCHER, A. G. *Invertebrate Fossils.* New York: McGraw-Hill, 1952.

SHIMER, HERVEY W. AND SCHROCK, R. R. *Index Fossils of North America.* New York: John Wiley & Sons, 1944.

SHROCK, R. R. AND TWENHOFEL, W. H. *Invertebrate Paleontology.* New York: McGraw-Hill, 1952.

Vertebrates

COLBERT, E. H. *The Dinosaur Book.* New York: American Museum of Natural History, 1945.

COLBERT, E. H. *Evolution of the Vertebrates.* New York: John Wiley & Sons, 1955.

HAY, O. P. *The Pleistocene of the Middle Region of North America and its Vertebrate Animals.* Washington, D.C.: Carnegie Inst. of Washington, Publication No. 332A, 1924.

ROMER, A. S. *Vertebrate Paleontology.* Chicago: University of Chicago Press, 1945.

Plants

ANDREWS, H. N., JR. *Ancient Plants and the World They Lived In.* Ithaca: Comstock Publ. Co., 1947.

ARNOLD, C. A. *An Introduction to Paleobotany.* New York: McGraw-Hill, 1947.

WALTON, JOHN. *An Introduction to the Study of Fossil Plants.* Adam and Charles Black. London, 1953.

Plate 1

Figure 1. Graptolites. Five fragmentary specimens of uncrushed graptolites from the Maquoketa shale (Ordovician) in Jefferson County, Missouri. Magnified three times.

Figure 2. *Receptaculites*. This is one of the so called "sunflower corals" which is probably not a true coral. This picture is natural size but many specimens are more than a foot in diameter. These are common in the Kimmswick formation (Ordovician).

Figure 3 & 4. Fusulinids. Fig. 3 shows a piece of limestone containing these "wheat grain" fossils. Magnified times two. Fig. 4 is a transverse section through one of the fusulinids showing the coiled structure of the shell. Magnified about 15 times. (Fig. 4 courtesy of C. H. Johnson).

Figure 5. *Stromatopora*. A polished vertical section showing the layered structure of part of a well-preserved colony from Callaway limestone (Devonian). Natural size.

Plate 2

CORALS

Figure 1. *Streptelasma.* A common "horn coral" which ranges from Ordovician to Devonian in age. Natural size.

Figure 2. *Zaphrentis.* Another common "horn coral" which ranges from Silurian to Mississippian in age. Natural size.

Figure 3. *Lophophyllidium.* A small solitary coral from Pennsylvanian rocks. Magnified times two.

Figure 4. *Triplophyllum.* A solitary Mississippian coral which is similar to *Zaphrentis* but is spiny. Natural size.

Figure 5. *Cystiphyllum.* A solitary Devonian coral characterized by the absence of well-defined septa and a great abundance of foam-like tissue. Natural size.

Figure 6. *Favosites.* A colonial tabulate Devonian coral with small corallites. Natural size.

Figure 7. *Chaetetes.* A small portion of a colony of another tabulate coral, commonly called the "hair coral." This photo is enlarged about five times.

BRYOZOA

Figure 8. Bryozoa. These two specimens are typical of many fragments of branching colonies. Each little pit represents the position of an individual animal. Magnification times two. These are from Pennsylvanian beds but similar forms also occur in beds of other ages.

Figure 9. *Evactinopora.* Some bryozoa built colonial skeletons in this star-like form. These are common in some Mississippian beds of Missouri. Natural size.

Plate 3
CORALS

Figure 1. *Aulopora*. A small colony of the "creeping coral" attached to a brachiopod shell. Magnified times two. This genus ranges from Silurian to Pennsylvanian in age.

Figure 2. *Favistella*. A common colonial coral from Ordovician rocks. Natural size.

Figure 3. *Halysites*. The colonial coral commonly called "chain coral." This form is common in Silurian coral reefs. Natural size.

Figures 4, 5. *Zaphrentis*. A very well preserved Mississippian specimen which shows a view looking down into calyx. The depression in the upper part of the picture is called a *fossula*. Note the radial arrangement of the septa. Natural size.

Figure 6. *Amplexus*. A coral that is fairly common in the Burlington. Characterized by very short septa but well developed tabulae. Natural size.

BRYOZOA

Figure 7. *Bryozoa*. A small portion of a colony of Mississippian bryozoa commonly called the "lacy bryozoa." Natural size.

Figure 8. *Archimedes*. This corkscrew-like form represents the axis of a spirally-coiled colony of bryozoa. These are very abundant in certain beds of the Keokuk and younger Mississippian formations of Missouri. Natural size.

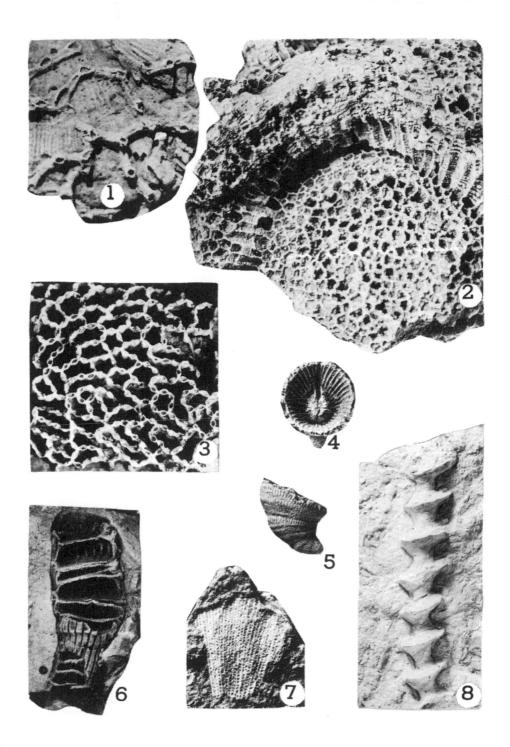

Plate 4

Figure 1. *Lithostrotionella.* A typical colony of coral which is common in the middle Mississippian of the eastern two-thirds of United States. Common in the St. Louis limestone of Missouri. Natural size.

Figure 2. *Hexagonaria.* Surface of a large colony of coral which is common in the middle Devonian all over the world, and very common in rocks of this age in Missouri. Each prismatic area represents the base of an individual animal. Natural size.

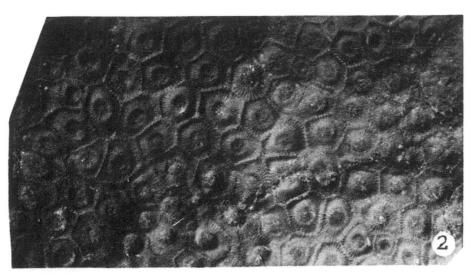

Plate 5

CRINOIDS

Figure 1. *Dorycrinus*. A fairly common form from the Burlington limestone. Natural size.

Figure 2. *Uperocrinus*. A basal view of a form that is also common in the Burlington. Natural size.

Figure 3. *Macrocrinus*. A small representative of a fairly common Burlington genus. Natural size.

Figure 4, 5, 7. *Batocrinus*. Three different species of a genus common in the lower half of the Mississippian. Natural size. (Figure 4 from Peck).

Figure 6. *Delocrinus*. Basal view of a form that is fairly common in Pennsylvanian beds. Natural size.

Figures 8 and 9. *Cactocrinus*. A common genus in the lower half of the Mississippian. Natural size. (From Peck).

Figures 16-19. Spines from Pennsylvanian crinoids. Natural size.

Figures 20, 21. Fragments of crinoid stems. Natural size.

Figure 24. Crinoid fragments. Photograph of the surface of a slab of Burlington limestone showing a large number of crinoid stem fragments. There is a crushed blastoid in the upper left. Natural size.

BLASTOIDS

Figures 10, 11. *Cryptoblastus*. A basal and side view of a specimen from the Chouteau (Mississippian) limestone. Natural size. (From Peck).

Figure 12. *Pentremites*. A well preserved typical specimen from the Mississippian of Missouri. Magnified times two.

Figure 13. *Metablastus*. A form from the Keokuk Mississippian limestone. Lateral view, natural size.

Figures 14, 15. *Cryptoblastus*. A basal and side view of a slightly flatter species than the one shown in Figures 10 and 11. Natural size. Also from the Chouteau. (From Peck).

ECHINOIDS

Figures 22, 23. Spines from Pennsylvanian echinoids. Natural size. These are very abundant in many Pennsylvanian beds. They vary considerably in shape and size.

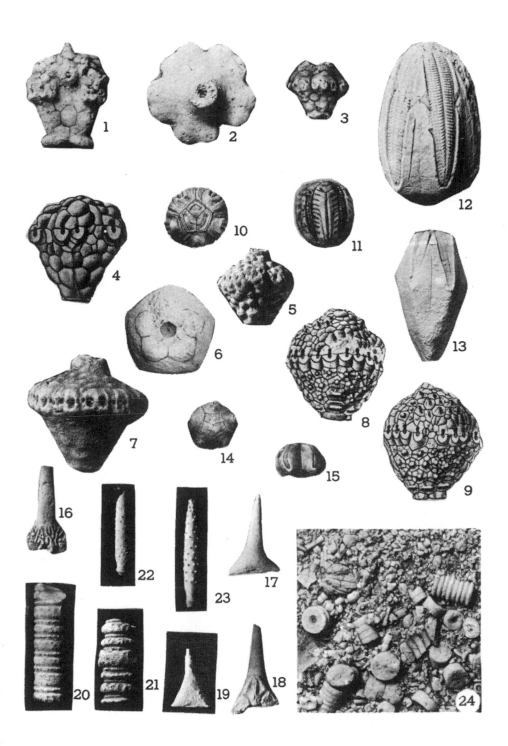

Plate 6
A portion of a slab of black Pennsylvanian shale from near Kansas City. On it can be seen the calyces, arms, and anal tubes of two specimens of *Aesiocrinus*.

(68)

Plate 7

ECHINOID

Figure 1. Drawing of a reconstructed echinoid from the St. Louis limestone near St. Louis which shows the arrangement of the skeletal plates. The spines have all been removed. (From Keyes).

Figure 2. Photograph of a similar specimen which came from the Burlington limestone near Ashland, Mo. This specimen was lent for illustration by Mr. Levi D. Harmon whose father found it about forty years ago. It remained an unidentified curio until recently.

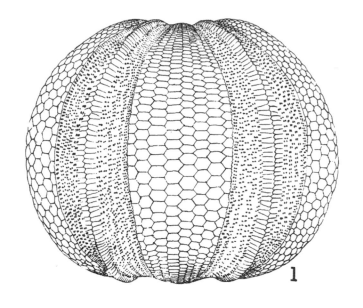

1

2

Plate 8

BRACHIOPODS

Figure 1. Orbiculoids. A drawing of a small piece of black shale on which are impressed the shells of several small orbiculoids. Natural size.

Figures 2 and 3. *Craenaena*. Two views of a small specimen from Devonian limestone. Natural size.

Figure 4. *Neospirifer*. A view showing the pedicle valve of a form common in Pennsylvanian beds. Natural size.

Figures 5 and 6. *Cyrtina*. Two views of a small genus which is common in many Devonian beds in Missouri. Natural size.

Figure 7. *Platyrachella*. A typical representative of this genus which is common in the Middle Devonian beds in Missouri. Natural size.

Figure 8. *Meekella*. A typical representative of a genus common in the Pennsylvanian in most of central United States. Natural size.

Figures 9 and 10. *Mucrospirifer*. Two views of a small Devonian species. Natural size.

Figure 11. *Dictyoclostus*. The pedicle valve of a genus very common in the Pennsylvanian of Missouri. Natural size. See also Plates 9 and 10.

Figures 12 and 13. *Composita*. Pedicle and lateral views of a genus that is common in Mississippian and Pennsylvanian beds of Missouri. Natural size.

Figure 14. *Crurithyris*. A common small genus in the Pennsylvanian. Magnified times two.

Figure 15. *Spirifer logani*. A view of the pedicle valve of a species which grows to large size and is common in the Keokuk limestone. This picture is slightly smaller than the specimen.

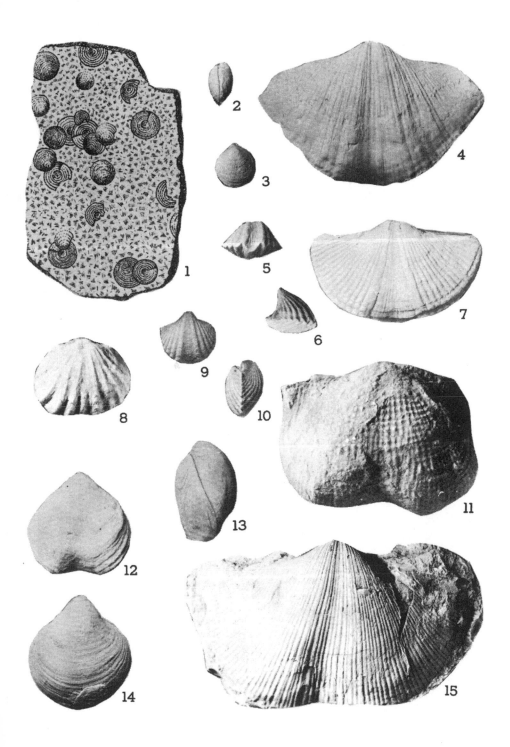

Plate 9

BRACHIOPODS

Figure 1. *Syringothyris*. View of cardinal area of typical specimen of this Mississippian genus. Natural size.

Figure 2. *Pionodema*. A small, finely striated genus which is common in the Ordovician beds of eastern Missouri. Magnified times two.

Figure 3. *Dictyoclostus*. View showing inside of brachial valve upon which is the coiled support for the feeding organ (lophophore). Natural size.

Figure 4. *Derbyia*. A very well preserved, large specimen of a genus which is common in the Pennsylvanian beds. This shows the pedicle valve which is usually very thin and fragile. Natural size.

Figure 5. *Marginifera*. A small form which is similar to *Dictyoclostus* but smaller. Fairly common in the Pennsylvanian. Natural size.

Figure 6 and 7. *Stropheodonta*. Brachial and pedicle views of a specimen from the Devonian. This genus is rather common in the Devonian beds and varies somewhat in outline and in convexity of the shell. Natural size.

Figure 8. *Echinoconchus*. A common, fairly large, genus from the Pennsylvanian. This genus is also represented in Mississippian beds. The small bumps all over the shell are the bases of small spines. Natural size.

Plate 10

BRACHIOPODS

Figure 1. *Dictyoclostus*. Pedicle valve of a fairly typical large specimen from Pennsylvanian beds in Missouri. Natural size.

Figure 2. *Linoproductus*. A typical Pennsylvanian form which is relatively free of spines. Natural size.

Figure 3. *Linoproductus*. A larger species than Figure 2, and one which is more spiny. The small bumps on the shell are spine bases. Natural size.

Figure 4. *Strophomena*. A common Ordovician genus which is characterized by the straight hinge line and thin cross section of the shell. Magnified times two, but many specimens are larger.

Figure 5. *Dictyoclostus*. Pedicle valve of a small Pennsylvanian specimen. More spiny than the one in Figure 1. Natural size.

Figure 6. *Dictyoclostus*. Brachial valve of a typical Mississippian member of this genus. Natural size.

Figure 7. *Orthotetes*. A fairly large genus which is well-represented in the Keokuk formation. This specimen is an internal mold and shows that the ornamentation of the shell affects the inside. Natural size.

Plate 11

BRACHIOPODS

Figures 1 and 2. *Platyrachella*. Interior and exterior views of a well preserved shell from the Devonian of central Missouri. Natural size.

Figure 3. *Composita*. View taken from brachial valve side of a Pennsylvanian specimen which shows the overlapping pedicle valve and the pedicle opening. Natural size.

Figure 4. A very small spiriferoid form from the Middle Devonian limestone of central Missouri. Magnified times two.

Figures 5 and 6. *Atrypa*. Side and top views of a typical specimen of a genus that is very common in the Devonian of Missouri. Natural size.

Figures 7 and 8. *Atrypa*. Two views of another specimen of this genus with well developed growth lines. Natural size.

Figure 9. *Atrypa*. A small specimen of this genus. Natural size.

Figure 10. *Leptaena*. A very distinctive genus which has a rather long time range. The illustrated specimen is from the Mississippian but the genus is also known from Silurian and Devonian. Natural size.

Figure 11. *Mesolobus*. A small genus characteristic of the middle Pennsylvanian rocks. Easily recognized by the middle lobe in the shell. Magnified times two.

Figure 12. *Dictyoclostus*. A typical Mississippian representative of this genus. Natural size.

Figure 13. *Resserella*. A typical specimen of a genus that is very common in the Upper Ordovician beds in Missouri. Magnified times two.

Figure 14. *Camarotoechia*. A small distinctive genus which ranges from Silurian to Mississippian in age. Magnified times two.

Figures 15 and 26. *Stropheodonta*. Small representatives of a common Devonian genus. Natural size.

Figures 16 and 17. *Spirifer*. Two views of a small specimen of a rather common Devonian form. Natural size.

Figure 18. *Productella*. A small spinose form which is believed to be the ancestor of most of the later spiny brachiopods. Natural size.

Figure 19. *Stropheodonta*. A small specimen of this common Devonian genus. Natural size.

Figure 20. *Chonetes*. A very distinctive genus which ranges from Silurian to Pennsylvanian. Some species are very useful as index fossils in the Pennsylvanian. Note the small spine bases along the hinge line. Magnified times two.

Figure 21. *Juresania*. A very spinose form common in Pennsylvanian and Permian rocks. Natural size.

Figure 22. *Dielasma*. A typical representative of a smooth-shelled genus from Mississippian rocks. Natural size.

Figure 23. *Derbyia*. A small specimen of a genus that is fairly common in the Pennsylvanian of Missouri. See also Plate 8.

Figure 24. *Phricodothyris*. A common small genus in Pennsylvanian limestones. Natural size.

Figure 25. *Reticularia*. A finely spiny genus from the Burlington limestone. Natural size.

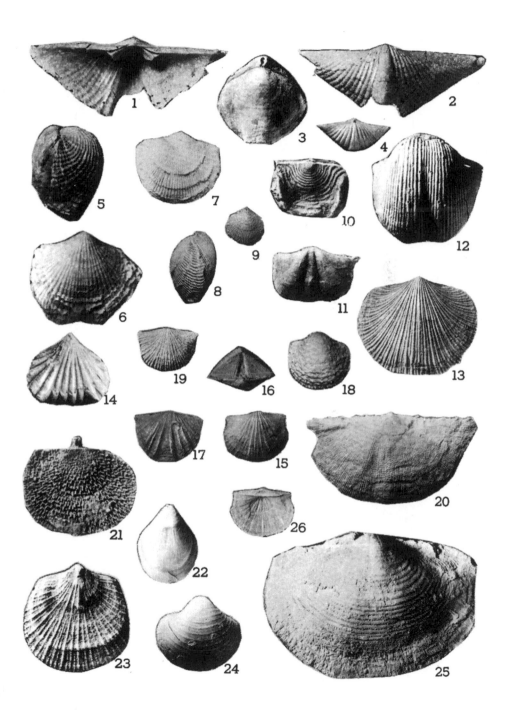

Plate 12

GASTROPODS

Figure 1. *Naticopsis.* View looking down upon the apex of an average-size specimen from the Pennsylvanian of western Missouri. Natural size.

Figure 2. *Platyceras.* Internal mold of a small specimen from the Burlington formation. Natural size.

Figure 3. *Hormotoma.* This genus is fairly common in the Ordovician and is abundant in some parts of the Kimmswick and Plattin formations of Missouri. It is nearly always preserved as an internal mold of the coiled shell. Natural size.

Figure 4. *Platystoma.* A typical representative from the Devonian. This is also an internal mold of the shell. Natural size.

CEPHALOPODS (Nautiloid)

Figures 5 and 6. *Solenochilus.* A typical representative of this genus which is fairly common in the Pennsylvanian of the mid-continent region. Natural size.

Plate 13

Figure 1. "Shark tooth." This specimen is typical of the so-called "pavement type" of fish teeth found in the Mississippian and Devonian of Missouri. This specimen is from the Burlington. Natural size.

Figure 2. *Meekospira.* A small gastropod genus common in the shales above the coals in the Pennsylvanian. Natural size.

Figure 3. and 4. *Pharkindonotus.* A fairly common gastropod in the Pennsylvanian limestones and shales. Natural size.

Figures 5 and 6. *Trepospira.* Two views looking down upon the apex of this slightly flattened coiled gastropod from the Pennsylvanian shale and limestone. Natural size.

Figure 7. *Leptotygma.* Typical representative gastropod genus of the middle Pennsylvanian. Natural size.

Figure 8. *Strobeus.* A fairly common gastropod in the Pennsylvanian beds of the Mississippi valley. Natural size.

Figure 9. *Amphiscapha.* A plano-spiral form from beds of Pennsylvanian age. Natural size.

Figure 10. *Euomphalus.* A well-preserved gastropod from the Burlington limestone. Natural size.

Figure 11. *Gomphoceras.* A large straight cephalopod from the Devonian. This picture is about one-third natural size.

Figure 12. *Allorisma.* A pelecypod (clam) that is fairly common in many Pennsylvanian shales and limestones. Natural size.

Plate 14

TRILOBITES

Figure 1. *Isotelus.* A common Ordovician genus. This excellent specimen is from the Kimmswick of eastern Missouri. The picture is about one-half the size of the specimen.

Figure 2. *Ameura.* The pygidium (tail) of a genus common in Pennsylvanian rocks in Missouri. The tail is the part most often found. Natural size.

Figure 3. *Phillipsia.* This small genus is fairly common in the lower Mississippian. Generally, however, only the tails are found. This is an unusually well-preserved specimen from northeast of Columbia. Magnified times two.

Figure 4. *Bumastus.* A very well preserved specimen from the Kimmswick of eastern Missouri. Natural size.

Figure 5. *Calymene.* A very common trilobite in Silurian rocks. Natural size.

Figure 6. Trilobites and Bryozoa. A small piece of shaly limestone from the upper part of the Plattin formation near Eureka, Mo., showing several trilobite pygidia and fragments of branching bryozoa. Natural size.

(85)

WORMS

Figure 1. *Scalarituba*. An impression of a flattened annulated worm which was buried in soft mud which later hardened to form the Hannibal shale. Similar forms occur in the Northview formation. Natural size.

Figure 2. *Taonurus caudagalli*. These markings are common in many shaly and silty formations and have been thought to be caused by worms. Their exact origin is not known. Natural size illustration, but the size of various specimens ranges widely.

PLANTS

Figure 3. *Calamites*. A portion of a plant stem of Pennsylvanian age. This plant is closely related to the modern horsetail rush. The size of these plants reached large dimensions, some being as much as 100 feet tall in Pennsylvanian time. Natural size illustration.

Figure 4. *Sigillaria*. Imprint of portion of a Pennsylvanian "scale tree" trunk or limb. Natural size.

Figure 5. Carbon-film impression of a Pennsylvanian fern leaf in shale associated a coal bed. Natural size.

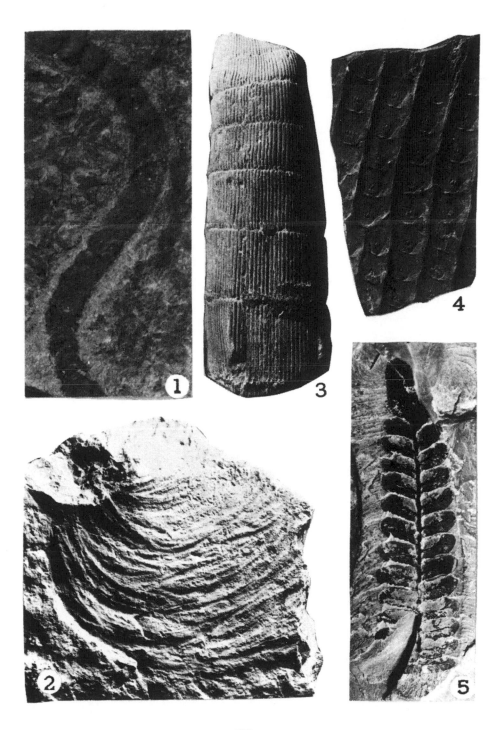

Plate 16

OSTRACODES

Figures 1-6. Representative specimens of ostracod shells. Figures 1 and 2 are of the genus *Bairdia*, Figure 3 of *Silenites*, Figure 4 of *Paraparchites*, and 5 and 6 are interior views of specimens of *Graphiodactylus*. All are magnified times twenty. (Photos after Morey.)

AMMONOIDS (goniatites)

The angular lines of these specimens represent the edges of the partitions which divide the shell into chambers.

Figures 7-10. *Eoasianites*. Typical representatives of a rather common Pennsylvanian genus. Natural size.

Figures 11-13. *Anthracoceras*. A very typical Pennsylvanian goniatite genus. Magnified times two.

Figure 14. *Neoglyphioceras*. A Pennsylvanian genus characterized by the longitudinal ridges on the shell. Magnified times two.

Figures 15 and 16. *Gonioloboceras*. Two views of a well preserved specimen from the Pennsylvanian of Henry County, Missouri. Magnified times two.

(All goniatite photos after Miller and Owen.)

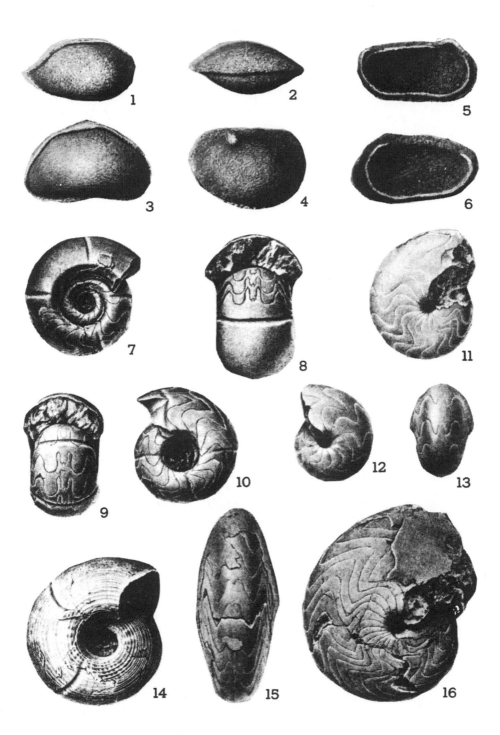

Plate 17

PSEUDOFOSSILS

Figure 1. Septarian concretion, formed by the shrinking and cracking of a ball of mud in which the cracks were later filled with some other substance. These are often mistaken for fossil turtles. Natural size.

Figure 2. Markings on the surface of a bed of siltstone. The actual cause of these is not well known but they are often mistaken for the impressions of the skin of an animal. Natural size.

Figures 3-5. Three views of a small siliceous concretion which bears a striking resemblance to an acorn. Magnified times two.

Figure 6. A sandstone concretion. These concretions are numerous and highly varied in form and are often thought to be the skeletal remains of some sort of animal. Natural size.

Figure 7. A limy concretion from a bed of loess. Concretions of this kind are highly varied in form and many of them resemble kewpies or dolls. Because of their shape they have been given the name "loesskindern" which means "children of the loess." Natural size.

Figure 8. Dendrites. Features of this sort are sometimes thought to be impressions of plants. However, they are formed by ground water permeating very thin openings in the rocks and leaving a thin branching deposit of some mineral. Natural size.

GLOSSARY AND PRONUNCIATION GUIDE
(Terms not defined here are defined in the text)

Algae (al' jee). Plants of very primitive structure, such as modern seaweed and pond scums.

Amber (am' ber). A yellowish fossilized plant resin.

Ambulacrum (am' bu la' krum). One of the radial zones of perforated plates in the echinoderms.

Ammonite (am' mon ite). Cephalopod with complexly wrinkled edges on the septa.

Amphibian (am fib' e an). Class of vertebrates which lay eggs in water and whose young go through an aquatic stage before becoming air-breathing adults.

Amphineura (am' fuh nur' uh). Molluscs in which the shell consists of more than two pieces.

Annelida (an nel' i duh). The segmented worms such as the common earthworm.

Anthozoa (an tho zo' a). A class of the Coelenterata which contains the sea anemones and corals.

Aquatic (uh kwat' ik). Pertaining to, living in, or growing in water.

Arachnid (uh rak' nid). Class of arthropods which includes the spiders, scorpions, and allies.

Archaeozoic (ar' kee o zo' ik).

Archimedes (ar kuh mee' deez).

Arthropod (ar' thro pod'). Invertebrate animal with jointed legs.

Articulate (ar tik' u late). Used here to refer to the hinge-like arrangement of parts of a skeleton.

Auloporidae (all' uh pore uh dee).

Blastoid (blast' oid). The echinoderm whose calyx is composed of thirteen plates.

Brachia (brake' ee uh). The arms of a crinoid, or the parts of the lophophore of a brachiopod.

Brachiopod (brak' ee o pod).

Bryozoan (bry' o zo' un). Small aquatic animal growing in colonies which have a moss-like appearance.

Calcareous (kal ka' re us). Composed of, containing or of the nature of calcium carbonate; limy.

Calyx (kay' lix). The part of a crinoid which contains most of the soft part of the animal. Also used to denote the upper part of the skeleton of a horn coral.

Cambrian (kam' bree uhn). The first period of the Paleozoic Era.

Camera (kam' er uh). The space between septa in the cephalopods.

Cenozoic (sen' o zo ik).

Cephalon (sef' uh lon). The head or front part of a trilobite.

Cephalopod (sef' uh lo pod).

Chara (kara). Primitive plants which produce their fruits in small calcified spheres.

Chert (churt). A rock composed of silicon dioxide; sometimes called flint.
Chitin (ki' tun). A horny substance which composes the shells of crustacea, similar to the human finger nail.
Chiton (ki' tun). A mollusc which has a shell composed of eight segments, sometimes called "sea mouse."
Cirri (sear' ee). Jointed appendages on crinoid stems.
Coelenterata (se len' ter ah ta). The phylum having a gastric cavity occupying the entire interior part of the body. Includes corals, jellyfish, etc.
Colonial (ko lo' ni al). Refers to the way in which many animals live in close association and share parts of their body walls. Biologically this word does not mean exactly the same as it does in general usage.
Column (kol' um). The stalk in crinoids.
Columnal (kol um' nal). The separate disks from which the crinoid column is built.
Conodonts (cone' o dont). Small tooth-like fossils which resemble fish teeth.
Corallite (kor' al lite). The skeleton of an individual coral.
Corallum (ko ral' um). The skeleton of a colony of corals.
Cretaceous (kree ta' shus).
Crinoid (cri' noid).
Crustacea (crus ta' cea). A class of arthropods having crust-like shells.
Cystoid (sis' toid).

Deciduous (de sid' yu us). Used here to refer to trees which shed their leaves seasonally.
Detrital (de tri' tul). Composed of loose fragments or particles.
Devonian (de vo' ni an).
Dolomite (dawl' o mite). A rock composed of the carbonates of calcium and magnesium being dominant.

Echinoderm (e ki' no durm).
Echinoid (ek' uh noid). A sea animal of bun or disc shape covered with spines; commonly called sea urchin.
Echinoidea (ek uh noi dea).
Edrioasteroidea (e' dree o as ter oi' de a).
Endothyroid (en' do thy' roid).

Fenestellate (fen' es tell' ate). Composed of or having the appearance of many small windows or openings.
Flint (see chert).
Foraminifera (fo ra min' i fer a).
Fusulinid (fyoo suh lin id).

Gastropod (gas' tro pod).
Genera (jen' er a). Plural of genus.
Genus (jee' nus). The group next above the species in classification; may include one or more species.
Graptolite (grap' toe lite).

Holdfast (hold' fast). The anchoring device at the base of a crinoid stem.
Holothuroidea (hol' o thu roid ea).
Hydrozoa (hy dro zo' a).

Igneous (ig' nee us). Pertaining to rocks formed from molten material.
Inarticulate (in ar tic' yu late). Not joined or attached by a hinge.
Invertebrate (in ver' tuh brate). Without a spinal column.

Jurassic (ju ras' ik).

Linguloid (ling' gyoo loid). Tongue-shaped.
Lophophore (lo' fo fore). Feeding and breathing organ in the brachiopods and in the Bryozoa.

Mesozoic (mes' o zoic).
Metamorphic (met uh morf' ik). Changed in form. In rocks it refers to a change in mineral composition caused by heat, pressure, or chemical change.
Metamorphosis (met uh mor' fuh sis). Passing from one shape or form to another. Applied to the life history of the insects as they change from egg to larva to cocoon to adult.
Miocene (my' o seen).
Mollusca (mol lus ka). Phylum of unsegmented, soft-bodied invertebrates typically protected by a calcareous shell. Includes clams, snails, etc.

Nautiloidea (nau' tuh loid ea).
Notochord (no' tow cord). Primitive spinal column in early forms of vertebrates.

Octopoda (oc' tuh pode uh).
Oligocene (ol' uh go seen).
Operculum (o per' qu lum). Horny or shelly plate used to cover the opening in snail shells.
Ordovician (or' doe vish un).
Organism (or' gan ism). An organized living being, animal or plant.

Paleozoic (pale' o zoic).
Pedicle (ped' ee kul). The stalk by which brachiopods are attached.
Pelecypod (pell ess' uh pod). A bi-valved mollusc, clam.
Phylum (phy' lum). A division of a kingdom, plant or animal.
Pleistocene (plice' tuh seen).
Pliocene (ply' o seen).
Porifera (po rif' er a).
Porphyry (por' fi ri). An igneous rock in which a fine-grained mass encloses larger crystals.
Proterozoic (prot er o zo' ik).
Protoconch (pro' to konk). The first stage in growth of a mollusc shell.
Protozoa (pro' to zo' a).
Pygidium (puh jid' e um). Posterior portion, or tail, of an insect or crustacean.

Radiolaria (ra di o la' ri a).

Rhyolite (rye' o lite). An igneous rock with glassy or nearly glassy texture.

Sauropod (sar' o pod). Amphibious four-footed dinosaur.

Scaphopoda (scaf' o pod a).

Scyphozoa (sy fo zo' a). Class of coelenterates containing jellyfish.

Septa (sep' tuh). Dividing walls separating shells into chambers.

Sigillaria (sij' uh la' ri a).

Solitary (sol' uh tary). Living alone. In zoological usage it means not a part of a colony.

Spicule (spick' yool). Small needle-like growth of calcite or silica serving as a stiffening in soft tissues of sponges or other invertebrates.

Spore (spor). The reproductive body in flowerless plants.

Terrestrial (ter res' tree ul). As used here, applies to sediments deposited upon the land surface.

Thorax (tho' rax). The part of the body between the neck and abdomen.

Trichina (tri kee' unh). A parasitic worm that sometimes infests the muscles of man and swine.

Trilobite (try' lo bite).

Valve (valv). One of the parts of a shell.

Vertebrata (ver' tuh bra tuh).

Viscera (vis' er uh). Internal organs of an animal.